Around the world in

Around the world in

80bites

Savour the aromas and flavours of 80 of the world's

greatest snacks, bites, mezze and tapas!

Sunil Vijayakar

hamlyn

To Lou, Evan, Colin and Gregg.

First published in Great Britain in 2005 by
Hamlyn, a division of Octopus Publishing Group Ltd
2–4 Heron Quays, London E14 4JP

ISBN 0 600 61312 7
EAN 9780600613121

A CIP catalogue record for this book is available from
the British Library

Printed and bound in China

10 9 8 7 6 5 4 3 2 1

NOTES

Both metric and imperial measurements have been
given in all recipes. Use one set of measurements
only, and not a mixture of both.

The Department of Health advises that eggs should
not be consumed raw. This book contains dishes made
with raw or lightly cooked eggs. It is prudent for more
vulnerable people such as pregnant and nursing
mothers, invalids, the elderly, babies and young
children to avoid uncooked or lightly cooked dishes
made with eggs. Once prepared, these dishes should
be kept refrigerated and used promptly.

Pepper should be freshly ground black pepper unless
otherwise stated.

Fresh herbs should be used, unless otherwise stated.

Ovens should be preheated to the specified
temperature – if using a fan-assisted oven, follow the
manufacturer's instructions for adjusting the time and
the temperature.

CONTENTS

INTRODUCTION

6 **The world on a plate**

The world is a fascinating place, not least because of the diversity of its countries and their respective cultures. And if there is one element of a country that typifies its cultural, historical and social uniqueness more tellingly than any other, it has to be its food. At its most basic, food is essential for survival; however, it can also be a great pleasure. The cuisines of countries around the globe have developed as much in response to this secondary factor, as they have to the first. The social element of eating and drinking has brought families and friends together to celebrate, enemies together to negotiate and leaders together to contemplate, since humans first roamed the planet. Sharing food is a bonding ritual that can overcome language barriers and cultural disparities; by sampling the typical food of a country or region you are at the same moment stepping back in time and immersing yourself in the history of that place. Knowledge of a country's cuisine is an essential part of the knowledge of the country itself, and the stories behind the recipes can be as interesting as the dishes themselves, with many steeped in ancient tradition.

Variations on a theme

The abundance of indigenous ingredients in certain countries resulted in the development of dishes to use them, but from meat through to breads and sauces, similar dishes are interpreted very differently, depending on the other ingredients available. Bread of some description is a staple food in many countries, yet there are significant variations in appearance, texture and cooking techniques, depending on where you travel. Irish soda bread (Smoked Salmon and Gubbeen Bites, page 21) uses bicarbonate of soda as a leavening agent because the bread was first baked before yeast was widely used; German rye bread (Beefsteak Tartare on Endive Scoops variation, page 26) is made with rye flour rather than wheat; while the Mexican tortilla (Spinach and Pepper Quesadilla Wedges, page 120) was traditionally made from corn, a predominant crop in that part of the world.

Trading tastes

Although individual ingredients in typical recipes are often native to the country, this is not always the case. Many well-

known dishes have resulted from trade, immigration or exploration, with the introduction of new foods and cooking methods to a country that were subsequently adopted into its storecupboard. For example, the potato, unheard of in Europe until Sir Walter Raleigh brought some back from Virginia to Great Britain in the 1590s, was soon introduced into the repertoire of cooks around the continent and now features heavily in typical dishes of many European countries, particularly Ireland and England (Crispy Whitebait and Mini Chip Cones, page 25). Another example is the classic American hot dog (New York-style Hot Dogs, page 172) – German immigrants brought their taste for sausages with them to the USA in the early 1800s and began to sell them as a quick snack from carts on the street. The rest, as they say, is history!

Sugar and spice
The item that has probably had the greatest impact on cuisine around the world is sugar. First brought to England in the 14th century, sugar had by then already had a long history, having been imported from its native Pacific islands'

home to India and other parts of Asia before reaching mainland Europe. As its popularity increased and sugar cane production expanded to cope with demand, there followed a tarnished period in sugar's history. Sugar cane was one of the crops that relied almost entirely on slave labour, and millions of Africans were forcibly removed from their homes or sold by local slave owners and transported to the new plantations in the Caribbean, in order to work for and line the pockets of European traders. As sugar became more widely available, its price dropped and it became a common foodstuff rather than the prized luxury of previous years.

Other ingredients that were rare and highly expensive when first introduced to the Western world were spices; although taken for granted these days, there was a time when peppercorns were counted out and sold individually. There was intense competition amongst many European countries for mastery of the spice trade and this required control over the spice-producing countries (this was the impetus for Christopher Columbus to set out on the voyage that led to the discovery of

America). Eventually England was established as the country in control of this precious trade, which brought with it substantial wealth and power. As with sugar, once spices became more readily available, they were used in a variety of recipes as a flavouring for meat, poultry and desserts.

Growth of trade

An increase in trade between nations, and advances in transport, meant that food could be moved between countries quickly and effectively, while the introduction of exotic ingredients into mainstream European cooking resulted in an increased awareness and interest in food, as people sampled the cuisines of other countries for the first time. It seems strange to think that not long before 1600, no one outside the Americas had ever seen a tomato or potato, yet these were to become two of the basic staple foods in European cooking and were so successful because they flourished in the colder climate.

Despite the steadily increasing trade between Europe and the Americas, it was not just in Europe that new foods were introduced. As ships docked to fill the stores with exotic spices and seedlings, other products would be offloaded or traded, and produce and animals would find themselves in new homes. Early settlers in the Americas brought the seeds of favourite crops with them, whilst the slave trade also had a major impact on food and eating habits – transporting foods and seeds from West Africa to the Caribbean and the Americas, where crops, such as okra, were successfully cultivated and became an integral part of the emergent cuisine of those regions.

The great divide

Although many recipes are traditional throughout the length and breadth of a country, there are almost always regional specialities, again dependent on the ingredients specific to customs and cultural variations existing within different regions. In the days when transport was difficult or even non-existent, people travelled very rarely and usually only out of necessity, and thus specialized dishes remained specific to their region. Cheese is one such product that remains highly regional, with independent cheese-makers maintaining age-old recipes and methods. Other examples include the pasta and risotto dishes of Italy, which vary greatly between the regions, or the vastly different cuisines of the United States. You'll find regional dishes or variations of national dishes in most countries and sampling them can be one of the most rewarding and memorable aspects of travelling in a foreign country.

Bite-sized samples
As well as regional culinary variations, many countries have a strong tradition of street food, and in a book of bite-sized portions it's worth mentioning this phenomenon. Essentially what is being created on the street is a miniature taster of some of the elements of a country's typical food – giving you an idea of the ingredients and cooking techniques that are used and the combinations of flavours that go into typical dishes of that country. From the hot dogs of New York to the samosas of India, street food is a split-second culinary tour that should not only appease hunger but rather assault all the senses at once – smell, taste, sight, touch and hearing should all be treated to the experience. Food stalls are a place for people to gather, gossip and grab a bite to eat. The food markets of countries such as Singapore and Thailand go one step further, since every conceivable local and national dish is on offer. At first the huge choice can be disconcerting, but it becomes immensely enjoyable once you've succumbed to the mouth-watering aromas and the constant barrage of noise. There is something very comforting about people meeting to eat and talk; it is perhaps why entertaining, more often than not, involves food. Spanish tapas and Greek mezze both work on the principle of little tasters of dishes – food that can be shared. The Swedish smörgåsbord is a similar concept and other variations exist around the world. Whether it's the way the bread is cooked, the way the meat is cured or the exact combination of spices or other flavours used, every recipe is unique and has evolved through many years of preparation, adaptation and evolution. By sampling the dishes that follow, you will experience a taste of the cuisines of numerous countries around the world and a sense of the history behind their creation.

EUROPE

14 Herring and dilled-cucumber skewers

Using a vegetable peeler, cut the cucumber into long, thin slices and put them into a shallow, non-reactive bowl. Mix the vinegar with the sugar, stir in the dill and pour over the cucumber. Season well with salt and pepper, cover and leave to pickle in the refrigerator for 3–4 hours.

Meanwhile, make the dipping sauce. Finely grate the beetroot in a food processor or blender. Add the soured cream and mayonnaise and blend until fairly smooth and pink, then chill until ready to use.

To serve, thread a herring fillet on to a wooden or bamboo skewer with some of the cucumber slices. Repeat with the remaining herring and cucumber to give you 15 skewers. Serve at room temperature with the dipping sauce.

Makes 15

15 canned or bottled pickled herring (*matjes*) fillets, drained, or 15 rollmop herring fillets

Dilled cucumber
1 large cucumber
200 ml (7 fl oz) white wine vinegar
2 teaspoons caster sugar
3 tablespoons finely chopped dill
salt and pepper

Pink beetroot soured cream dipping sauce
50 g (2 oz) cooked, peeled beetroot
100 ml (3½ fl oz) soured cream
100 g (3½ oz) mayonnaise

The **smörgåsbord** is Sweden's most famous type of cuisine, where many different foods are served, buffet-style, at the table. This recipe recreates the tradition in miniature.

Rye, chive and cream cheese squares 17

Put the cream cheese and pickled cucumber into a small bowl and beat until smooth. Using a small palette knife, spread the mixture thickly on to the rye bread squares.

Using a very sharp knife or a very sharp pair of kitchen scissors, very finely chop the chives and spread on to a plate in a thick, even layer. Working carefully and neatly, dip each bread square, cream-cheese side down, into the chopped chives to coat it evenly with the chives. Put the bread, chive-side up, on a serving platter and arrange a slice of cucumber and red radish in the centre of each square. Season well with salt and pepper, garnish with more chives if desired and serve immediately.

Makes 20

250 g (8 oz) cream cheese
1 tablespoon very finely diced pickled cucumber
20 squares of very dark rye bread, cut into 3.5 cm (1½ inch) squares
large bunch of chives
20 very thin slices of cucumber
20 very thin slices of red radish
salt and pepper
extra chives, to garnish

Smorrebrod are open sandwiches that are traditionally served at lunchtime in Danish cafés. These are a bite-sized version.

18 Mini quail Scotch eggs

Put the eggs in a medium saucepan and cover with cold water. Bring to a boil, stirring gently to centre the yolks, then simmer for 4–5 minutes. Drain the eggs, then put under cold running water. When cool, carefully remove the shells and set the eggs aside.

Put the minced chicken, mustard, mint jelly and parsley in a bowl. Season with salt and pepper and mix well until thoroughly combined. Divide the mixture into 12 portions.

Toss the eggs in a little plain flour and shake off the excess. Using lightly floured hands, shape a portion of chicken mixture around each egg to form a neat ball. Dip each ball into the beaten egg, then roll in the breadcrumbs to coat evenly.

Pour the oil into a deep-fat fryer to a depth of at least 7 cm (3 inches) and heat to 180°C (350°F). Deep-fry the balls for 4–5 minutes until well browned, then drain on kitchen paper. When cool enough to handle, cut the balls in half and serve immediately or at room temperature.

Makes 24

12 quails' eggs
300 g (10 oz) finely minced chicken
1 teaspoon English mustard
1 teaspoon mint jelly
2 tablespoons finely chopped parsley
plain flour, for tossing
1 egg, lightly beaten
150 g (5 oz) natural dried breadcrumbs
sunflower oil, for deep-frying
salt and pepper

These little bites are lighter than traditional Scotch eggs, the tiny quails' eggs being covered with minced chicken instead of sausagemeat.

IRELAND

Smoked Salmon and Gubbeen Bites

Using a 2.5 cm (1 inch) round biscuit or pastry cutter, stamp out 20 rounds from the soda bread. Mix the butter with the mustard and spread it thickly over the bread rounds.

Using the cutter, stamp out 20 rounds of the Gubbeen and use to top the prepared bread rounds, then use the cutter to stamp out 20 rounds of the smoked salmon and put those on top of the cheese.

To serve, put the soda bread canapés on a serving platter and squeeze a little lemon juice over each one. Season with the pepper and serve immediately.

Makes 20

8–9 thin slices of Irish soda bread
100 g (3½ oz) butter, softened
1 tablespoon wholegrain mustard
400 g (13 oz) Irish Gubbeen cheese,
  thinly sliced
400 g (13 oz) Irish smoked salmon,
  thickly sliced

To serve
lemon juice
pepper

A pale cheese with a tough rind and crumbly texture, Gubbeen is made from cow's milk. The name refers to a bay in West Cork where the cheese is produced.

22 Goats' cheese and red pepper puffs

Lightly grease a baking sheet with sunflower oil and line with nonstick baking paper.

To make the puffs, bring the water, salt and butter to the boil in a pan over a medium heat. Remove from the heat, add the flour and stir with a wooden spoon until well mixed. Return to the heat and beat for 1–2 minutes, until the mixture is smooth and pulls away from the sides. Off the heat, beat in the eggs, one at a time, making sure each egg is mixed in before adding the next. Beat until the mixture is smooth and glossy (it will be slightly sticky).

Drop tablespoonfuls of the mixture on to the baking sheet and put in a preheated oven, 180°C (350°F), Gas Mark 4, for 25–30 minutes until puffed up.

Meanwhile, combine all the filling ingredients in a bowl.

To serve, remove the puffs from the oven and leave to cool. Split each one in half, spread a little cheese mixture on one half and top with the remaining half. Serve immediately.

Makes about 15

Puffs

sunflower oil, for greasing
175 ml (6 fl oz) water
pinch of salt
75 g (3 oz) butter
125 g (4 oz) plain flour, sifted
3 eggs

Filling

100 g (3 ½ oz) Welsh goats' cheese (soft)
2 tablespoons cream cheese
3 tablespoons very finely chopped roasted red pepper (use canned or bottled)
1 tablespoon finely chopped chives
salt and pepper to taste

Goats' cheeses can range from very soft and spreadable to hard and crumbly. Welsh goats' cheese is renowned for its flavour and quality.

Crispy whitebait and mini chip cones   **25**

Line a large sheet of newspaper with greaseproof paper, cut the double layer into 12 squares and twist each into a small cone.

Rinse the chips in cold water and dry thoroughly on kitchen paper. Pour the oil into a deep-fat fryer to a depth of at least 7 cm (3 inches) and heat to 180°C (350°F). Deep-fry the chips for 4–5 minutes, then drain on kitchen paper and deep-fry them again for 1–2 minutes until crisp and golden. Drain the chips and keep them warm in a preheated oven, 120°C (250°F), Gas Mark ½.

To prepare the whitebait, heat the oil to 180°C (350°F). Put the flour on a large plate and season well with salt and pepper. Toss the fish in the flour and fry in batches for 1–2 minutes, or until crisp and golden. Drain on kitchen paper.

To serve, toss the whitebait with the chips, season with sea salt and pile into the paper cones. Serve the malt vinegar on the side.

Makes 12 cones

Chips
**250 g (8 oz) potatoes, peeled and cut
into long, thin chips**
sunflower oil, for deep-frying
sea salt, for sprinkling
malt vinegar, to serve

Crispy whitebait
sunflower oil, for deep-frying
4 tablespoons plain flour
400 g (13 oz) whitebait
salt and pepper

The **great** British culinary tradition of **fish and chips** actually **originated** as two **separate entities**, with the **French inventing** the chips.

26 Beefsteak tartare on endive scoops

Using a very sharp knife, very finely chop the beef and then mince it (or get your butcher to do this for you).

Put the meat into a food processor with the capers, onions, parsley and anchovies and season well with pepper. Process until smooth.

Put the endive leaves on to a serving platter and spoon some of the tartare mixture on to the base of each leaf. Garnish with the parsley and serve the scoops immediately.

Variation

You could also serve the tartare mixture spooned on to dark rye bread, if desired.

Makes 20

200 g (7 oz) very good-quality, lean beef fillet steak

2 tablespoons capers, very finely chopped

2 tablespoons very finely chopped onion

2 tablespoons very finely chopped parsley

4 canned anchovy fillets, drained and finely chopped

pepper

20 green or red endive leaves

parsley, to garnish

Beef or **steak tartare** is meat that is **ground**, highly seasoned and **eaten raw**. The **crunchy endive** leaves provide a **good contrast** in texture.

Rosemary and veal frikadeller skewers   **29**

Cook the potato in a saucepan of lightly salted, boiling water for about 15 minutes until tender. Drain and put in a large bowl, then leave to cool.

Mash the potato, then stir in the rosemary, crème fraîche, anchovy paste, allspice, olive oil, breadcrumbs, red onion, garlic and veal. Season well with salt and pepper and mash to combine thoroughly. Divide the mixture into 25 portions and shape each one into a ball with your fingers. Arrange the balls on a nonstick baking sheet, cover with clingfilm and chill in the refrigerator for 2–3 hours.

When ready to cook the frikadellers, heat the oil in a large, nonstick frying pan to 160°C (325°F) and shallow-fry the balls, in batches, for 5–6 minutes, or until browned. Drain each batch on kitchen paper.

Remove some of the leaves from each rosemary sprig, leaving about 3.5 cm (1½ inches) of leaves untouched at one end. To serve, skewer the frikadeller with the rosemary stems and accompany with lemon wedges and a bowl of mayonnaise.

Makes 25

1 medium potato, peeled and roughly chopped
1 teaspoon very finely chopped rosemary leaves
1 tablespoon crème fraîche
1 teaspoon anchovy paste
¼ teaspoon ground allspice
1 tablespoon olive oil
3 tablespoons natural dried breadcrumbs
2 tablespoons very finely chopped red onion
1 garlic clove, crushed
350 g (11½ oz) finely minced veal
oil, for shallow-frying
salt and pepper

To serve
25 rosemary sprigs, 7–10 cm (3–4 inches) long
lemon wedges
mayonnaise

Frikadeller are **meatballs** and made here with veal, a **naturally** lean meat **popular** in Holland. Before it was used as a **flavouring** for meat, **rosemary** was primarily a **medicinal remedy** for infections.

30 Grilled mussels with herbed beer butter

Put the mussels into a large saucepan with the beer. Cover the pan, place over a high heat and cook for 4–5 minutes, shaking the pan from time to time to ensure the mussels cook evenly. When all the mussels have opened, remove the pan from the heat and discard the top shell from each mussel. Discard any mussels that have not opened. Put the mussels on a grill rack in a single layer and set aside.

Mix the butter with the parsley, lemon rind, juice and beer. Season well with salt and pepper and, using a small teaspoon, spoon some of the mixture on top of each mussel. Put the mussels under a medium-hot grill for 1–2 minutes, or until the butter has melted. Meanwhile, line a serving platter with sea salt – this will keep the mussels stable. Put the cooked mussels on the salt and serve immediately.

Makes 20

20 large, fresh mussels, scrubbed
100 ml (3½ fl oz) Belgian beer
sea salt, for lining platter

Herbed beer butter
100 g (3½ oz) butter, softened
4 tablespoons finely chopped parsley
1 teaspoon thinly grated lemon rind
2 tablespoons lemon juice
2 tablespoons Belgian beer
salt and pepper

The **distinctly** Belgian partnership of a **bowl** of **mussels** and a **tankard of beer** is well known. Here they're **combined** to make a **decadent snack**.

Seared foie gras on French bread

Put the bread under a medium grill and toast on both sides until crisp and lightly browned. Lightly rub one side of each slice of toast with the garlic and put on a serving platter, rubbed-side up.

Heat the oil in a large, nonstick frying pan until very hot. Add the foie gras and sear over a high heat for 2–3 minutes on each side. Remove the foie gras from the pan and, using a sharp knife, cut it into 12 slices. Put a slice on each piece of toast, season well with salt and pepper and sprinkle some chopped tarragon over each one to garnish. Serve immediately.

Makes 12

12 thin slices of bread cut from a small
   French baguette 5–6 cm (2–2½ inches)
   in diameter
3–4 garlic cloves, halved
1 tablespoon olive oil
3–4 slices of foie gras, 300–350 g
   (10–11½ oz) in total
salt and pepper
very finely chopped tarragon, to garnish

Despite being a French delicacy, foie gras is believed to have originated in Egypt. Today it is an expensive luxury food served on special occasions.

34 Reblochon, tomato and ham quichettes

Roll out the pastry on a lightly floured surface to a 2.5 mm (⅛ inch) thickness and use to line 20 mini tartlet tins 5–6 cm (2–2½ inches) in diameter. Prick the base of each quichette with a fork and chill for 30 minutes.

Line each tartlet case with nonstick baking paper and fill with baking beans. Put on a baking sheet in a preheated oven, 200°C (400°F), Gas Mark 6, for 11–12 minutes until firm, then remove the paper and beans and return to the oven for 8–10 minutes, or until crisp and golden. Remove from the oven and leave to cool on a wire rack.

Meanwhile, put the Reblochon in a freezer and chill until firm, then cut into as small dice as possible.

Divide the ham between the cooled quichette cases and top each one with cherry tomato quarters and the cheese. Return to the oven for 6–8 minutes, or until the cheese has melted and the tarts are golden. Remove from the oven and garnish with rosemary sprigs before serving.

Makes 20

300 g (10 oz) shortcrust pastry, thawed if frozen

Filling
150 g (5 oz) Reblochon cheese
3 tablespoons very finely chopped ham
8 cherry tomatoes, quartered
small rosemary sprigs, to garnish

Reblochon is a mild mountain cheese. The name refers to the creamy cow's milk that is specially selected for the production of the cheese.

Raclette fondue with baby potato dippers   **37**

Cook the potatoes in a large saucepan of lightly salted, boiling water for 10–12 minutes, or until just tender. Drain and set aside.

Rub the garlic around the interior of a medium-sized fondue pot. Discard the garlic. Put the Raclette and milk in the pot and heat gently over a low heat, stirring continuously with a wooden spoon. When the cheese starts to melt and the mixture becomes smooth and creamy, gradually add the wine and Kirsch. Season well with salt and pepper and heat the fondue through without boiling.

Use fondue forks or skewers to dip the boiled potatoes into the cheese mixture, and then eat them immediately.

Serves 4–6

750 g (1½ lb) baby new potatoes, scrubbed

2 garlic cloves, sliced in half

500 g (1 lb) Raclette cheese, diced

250 ml (8 fl oz) milk

200 ml (7 fl oz) dry white wine

1 tablespoon Kirsch

salt and white pepper

Harsh **winters** traditionally **isolated** many Swiss country people and when the summer **bread and cheese** became **dry and hard,** the **fondue** was **created** to make them **more enjoyable.**

38 Mini schinkenfleckerin

Break the noodles into small pieces about 3.5 cm (1½ inches) long and cook according to the packet instructions. Drain and set aside.

Line a 20 cm (8 inch) square, nonstick cake tin with nonstick baking paper.

Heat the butter and oil in a large frying pan and, when hot, add the onions. Cook, stirring, over a medium heat for 6–8 minutes until softened.

Whisk the eggs with the soured cream in a bowl. Stir in the ham, cooked noodles and onions, season well with salt and pepper and spoon the mixture into the prepared cake tin. Cover with foil and put in a preheated oven, 190°C (375°F), Gas Mark 5, for 45 minutes. Remove the foil and bake for another 10–15 minutes, or until the mixture is set and firm. Remove from the oven and leave to cool completely. To serve, cut into bite-sized squares.

Serves 4–6

200 g (7 oz) dried thin egg noodles
1 tablespoon butter
1 tablespoon olive oil
1 small onion, finely chopped
4 eggs, lightly beaten
6 tablespoons soured cream
200 g (7 oz) cooked ham, finely diced
salt and pepper

This **unusual combination** of cured ham and **noodles** is usually served as a casserole in Austria. **Some versions** are flavoured with spices.

Mini beef goulash and gherkin pies

Heat the oil in a nonstick pan over a medium heat and cook the onion, stirring, until softened. Increase the heat to high, add the beef and stir-fry until sealed and lightly browned.

Add the garlic, tomato purée, paprika and caraway seeds and cook, stirring, for 1–2 minutes. Add the stock and bring to the boil, then cover tightly and simmer over a very low heat for 2 hours, stirring occasionally. When the stock has reduced and the meat is very tender, remove from the heat and leave to cool completely. Stir in the soured cream and gherkins, season with salt and set aside.

Roll out the pastry to a 5 mm (¼ inch) thickness. Cut out 12 rounds with a 7 cm (3 inch) round cutter and 12 rounds with a 6 cm (2½ inch) cutter. Line a 12-hole mini muffin tin with the large rounds, and fill with teaspoons of the goulash. Cover the filling, pressing the edges to seal. Brush with beaten egg. Put in a preheated oven, 200°C (400°F), Gas Mark 6, for 30 minutes. Cool the pies on wire racks. Serve warm.

Makes 12

1 tablespoon olive oil

1 small onion, finely chopped

200 g (7 oz) beef fillet steak, cut into
   1 cm (½ inch) cubes

1 garlic clove, crushed

1 tablespoon tomato purée

1 tablespoon paprika

1 teaspoon caraway seeds

500 ml (17 fl oz) beef stock

1 tablespoon soured cream

1 tablespoon chopped gherkins

350 g (11½ oz) shortcrust pastry

beaten egg, for glazing

salt

Hungarian **herdsmen** traditionally prepared goulash as they drove their cattle to the **big markets** of Europe.

42 Blinis with soured cream and caviar

To make the blinis, sift the flours and salt into a large bowl and make a well in the centre. Whisk the egg yolk with the cream and milk and gradually pour into the well. Draw the flour into the egg mixture and mix to a smooth batter. Put the egg whites in a separate bowl and whisk until softly peaked, then, using a metal spoon, fold into the flour mixture and mix until just combined.

Brush a large, nonstick frying pan with a little oil and put over a medium heat. When hot, add heaped teaspoonfuls of the batter, in batches, and cook for about 3 minutes until bubbles appear on the surface. Flip the blinis over and cook for another 1–2 minutes, or until cooked through. Remove each batch from the pan and put on greaseproof paper to cool. Brush the pan with oil in between batches.

To serve, arrange the blinis on a serving platter and top with small spoonfuls of soured cream and caviar or roe. Just before serving, sprinkle the egg and the dill on the blinis, then season with pepper and serve.

Makes 20

Blinis
65 g (2½ oz) buckwheat flour
40 g (1½ oz) self-raising flour
pinch of salt
1 egg, separated
50 ml (2 fl oz) single cream
125 ml (4 fl oz) milk
sunflower oil, for frying

Topping
about 100 ml (3½ fl oz) thick, soured cream
150 g (5 oz) Russian caviar or salmon roe
1 tablespoon very finely chopped hard-boiled egg
1 tablespoon very finely chopped dill
pepper

Authentic caviar is the roe of the sturgeon; most caviar today comes from the Caspian Sea. In Russia, blinis (pancakes) are often accompanied by chilled vodka.

Courgette flower fritters

Carefully clean the courgette flowers and discard the stamens.

Sift the flour, baking powder and salt into a bowl. Gradually add the beer, whisking continuously until you have a smooth, slightly thick batter.

Heat the oil in a large, deep, heavy-based frying pan until it reaches 160°C (325°F). Working carefully and quickly, dip the courgette flowers into the batter, a few at a time, and lower into the hot oil. Fry each batch for 5–6 minutes, turning once, until lightly golden and crisp. Remove with a slotted spoon and drain on kitchen paper.

Serve the courgette flower fritters immediately, sprinkled with a little extra sea salt, if using.

Makes 15

15 courgette flowers
125 g (4 oz) very fine Italian plain flour (tipo O)
1 teaspoon baking powder
large pinch of salt
250 ml (8 fl oz) chilled beer
sunflower oil, for deep-frying
sea salt, for sprinkling (optional)

The life of a **courgette flower** is short and they are best prepared no more than two days after being harvested.

46 Proscuitto and scallop spiedini

Put the garlic into a small bowl, mix in the chilli, olive oil, orange juice and oregano and season with salt.

Arrange the scallops in a single layer in a shallow bowl and pour over the garlic and chilli mixture. Cover and leave to marinate for 15–20 minutes.

Cut each slice of proscuitto into 2 strips. Wrap a strip of proscuitto around each scallop and secure with a metal skewer or presoaked bamboo skewer. Add a basil leaf and a tomato half to each skewer.

Preheat the grill to high. Position the skewers about 6 cm (2½ inches) away from the grill and cook for 1–2 minutes on each side or until the scallops have just cooked through – do not overcook or the scallops will become tough.

Remove from the grill and serve immediately.

Makes 20

2 garlic cloves, crushed

1 dried red chilli, crushed

4 tablespoons olive oil

juice of ½ orange

1 teaspoon dried oregano

20 large scallops, with or without the coral (roe)

10 thin slices of proscuitto

salt

Garnish

20 basil leaves

20 sun-blushed tomato halves

Proscuitto is a **cured ham** that is **salted** for about two months before being hung until it has **dried completely**. Spiedini are Italian kebabs.

Manchego and membrillo bites

Cut the membrillo or quince cheese into 15 bite-sized cubes or pieces and set aside.

Put the egg whites in a clean bowl and, using an electric or rotary whisk, whisk until softly peaked. Fold in the Manchego, breadcrumbs and parsley, then season with salt and pepper and form the mixture into 15 bite-sized balls.

Heat the oil in a large, deep frying pan to 180°C (350°F) and fry the balls in batches for 2–3 minutes, or until golden brown and crisp. Drain on kitchen paper and keep each batch warm until all the balls have been cooked.

To serve, skewer a piece of the membrillo or quince cheese with a Manchego ball on a cocktail stick and serve immediately.

Makes 15

150 g (5 oz) membrillo or firm quince cheese

2 egg whites

125 g (4 oz) mature Manchego cheese, grated

75 g (3 oz) fresh white breadcrumbs

2 tablespoons finely chopped flat leaf parsley

sunflower oil, for deep-frying

salt and pepper

Manchego, made from sheep's milk, is the most well-known Spanish cheese. Membrillo is a jelly or paste made from quinces.

50 Green pea, potato and mint tortilla bites

Cook the potato in a saucepan of lightly salted, boiling water for about 15 minutes, or until just tender. Drain and set aside.

Heat the oil in a medium, nonstick frying pan over a medium heat and add the onion. Cook, stirring constantly, for 4–5 minutes, then add the garlic and drained potato. Cook, stirring, for 1–2 minutes, then add the peas and beaten eggs and season well with salt and pepper. Scatter in the mint. Turn the heat to low and cook for 10–12 minutes, or until the bottom of the tortilla is set and browned.

Put the tortilla under a medium-hot grill and cook until the top is set and lightly browned. Remove from the heat and leave to cool for 20 minutes before turning out on to a clean surface. Cut the tortilla into bite-sized squares, triangles or any other shapes you want and serve at room temperature.

Makes about 20

1 large potato, about 250 g (8 oz), peeled and cut into 1 cm (½ inch) squares
2 tablespoons Spanish olive oil
1 small onion, very finely chopped
1 garlic clove, finely chopped
400 g (13 oz) frozen peas, thawed
6 large eggs, lightly beaten
3 tablespoons chopped mint
salt and pepper

Regular tortillas are made only with eggs, while tortilla Espanola, or Spanish omelette, includes potatoes and is served in thick slices for breakfast or lunch.

Pecorino shortbread rounds with pesto   53

Line a baking sheet with nonstick baking paper. To make the shortbread rounds, sift the flour into a bowl and, using your fingers, mix in the paprika, butter and Pecorino until well combined. Knead for 4–5 minutes to form a smooth dough.

Roll out the dough on a lightly floured board to a 1 cm (½ inch) thickness and, using a 4 cm (1½ inch) round biscuit or pastry cutter, stamp out 20 rounds. Carefully put the rounds on the baking sheet and chill in the refrigerator for 1 hour.

Put the baking sheet in a preheated oven, 180°C (350°F), Gas Mark 4, for 8–10 minutes, or until the rounds are lightly browned. Remove from the oven and leave to cool on a wire rack until crisp and firm.

Meanwhile, put all the ingredients for the pesto in a food processor or blender and pulse to a thick paste.

To serve, put the shortbread rounds on a serving platter, top each one with a spoonful of the pesto and garnish with some diced tomato and a basil leaf.

Makes 20

Shortbread rounds
50 g (2 oz) plain flour, sifted
pinch of paprika
25 g (1 oz) cold butter, diced
40 g (1½ oz) finely grated Pecorino
   cheese

Pesto
1 garlic clove, crushed
20 g (¾ oz) basil
2 tablespoons pine nuts
5 tablespoons finely grated Pecorino
   cheese
2 tablespoons olive oil

Garnish
finely diced tomato
small basil leaves

Sardinia has a history of cheese-making and Pecorino, a hard cheese similar to Parmesan, is one of the country's specialities. Pesto originated in the Ligurian port of Genoa.

Greek filo and nut baklavas

To make the syrup, put all the ingredients into a pan and bring to the boil. Reduce the heat and simmer gently for 15 minutes until thickened slightly. Remove from the heat and leave to cool, then chill in the refrigerator for 4–5 hours or overnight.

To make the baklava, grease a 20 x 30 cm (8 x 12 inch) nonstick Swiss roll tin with the oil. Mix the nuts, cardamom and sugar. Brush 4 sheets of the filo with some melted butter and place on top of each other. Fold in half lengthways and use to line the prepared tin, trimming the pastry if necessary. Sprinkle one-third of the nut mixture over the filo, then repeat twice with the remaining filo and nut mixture to give 3 layers of nut mixture and 4 of filo. Brush the top with the remaining butter and score into large, bite-sized diamonds. Put in a preheated oven, 180°C (350°F), Gas Mark 4, for 30–35 minutes or until golden and crisp. Pour over the chilled syrup, then cover and refrigerate overnight.

To serve, cut the baklava into diamonds.

Serves 10–12

Spiced sugar syrup

500 g (1 lb) caster sugar
1/4 teaspoon ground cloves
1 teaspoon ground cinnamon
1 teaspoon thinly grated lemon rind
1 teaspoon thinly grated orange rind
500 ml (17 fl oz) water

Baklava

sunflower oil, for greasing
250 g (8 oz) almonds, finely chopped
200 g (7 oz) walnuts, finely chopped
1 teaspoon ground cardamom
125 g (4 oz) caster sugar
16 large sheets of filo pastry
175 g (6 oz) butter, melted

This **rich dish** with its **paper-thin pastry** was **being prepared** in the kitchens of Greece's **elite families** as long ago as 300BC.

AFRICA

58 Lemon and couscous-stuffed tomatoes

Cut the tomatoes in half and, using a small spoon, scoop out and discard the seeds. Put the tomato shells, cut-side down, on a piece of kitchen paper and set aside.

Put the couscous in a small heatproof bowl, stir in the oil and pour over boiling water to just cover. Cover with clingfilm and leave to rest for 8—10 minutes to absorb the water.

Meanwhile, finely dice the preserved lemon, discarding any seeds. Fluff up the couscous with a fork, stir in the lemon and mint and season well with salt and pepper.

Put the tomato halves on a serving platter. Using a small teaspoon, spoon some of the couscous mixture into each tomato shell, garnish with mint leaves, if using, and serve at room temperature.

Makes 20

10 midi tomatoes, each about 3.5 cm
(1½ inches) in diameter
50 g (2 oz) couscous
2 tablespoons olive oil
1 preserved lemon
3 tablespoons finely chopped mint
salt and pepper
tiny mint leaves, to garnish (optional)

Preserved lemons are used in all kinds of Moroccan dishes – they provide an almost creamy citrus flavour and go well with chicken, lamb and vegetables.

Crisp almond and sesame samsa

Bring 115 g (3¾ oz) of the sugar and all the water to the boil in a small pan. Reduce the heat to low and stir until the sugar has dissolved. Add the lemon juice, bring to the boil and boil rapidly for 10 minutes until syrupy. Remove from the heat and leave to cool. Stir in half the orange flower water.

Line a baking sheet with nonstick baking paper. Knead the ground almonds to a paste with the orange rind, cinnamon, the remaining sugar and orange flower water. Cut the filo into 24 long strips 6 cm (2½ inches) wide. Brush a strip with melted butter, put a small spoonful of almond filling at the bottom, fold over the sides and roll up the pastry along its length. Repeat with the remaining strips. Put the filo parcels on the baking sheet and brush with melted butter. Put in a preheated oven, 180°C (350°F), Gas Mark 4, for 15–18 minutes, until golden.

Remove the pastries from the oven and place in a single layer in a dish. Pour over the syrup and leave for 3–4 minutes. Lift the pastries on to a serving platter; sprinkle over the sesame seeds. Let cool.

Makes 24

150 g (5 oz) caster sugar
300 ml (½ pint) water
2 tablespoons lemon juice
2 tablespoons orange flower water
250 g (8 oz) ground almonds
thinly grated rind of 1 small orange
1½ teaspoons ground cinnamon
about 150 g (5 oz) filo pastry
melted butter, for brushing
4 tablespoons lightly toasted sesame
  seeds

Like most **North African pastries**, these crisp **samsa** from Tunisia are **very sweet**. Orange flower water is frequently used to flavour **pastries and desserts**.

62 Smoky aubergine dip with crudités

Using a pair of tongs to protect your hand, hold each aubergine over an open flame on the hob until lightly charred all over – each one will take about 10 minutes. Carefully put the aubergines on a nonstick baking sheet and put in a preheated oven, 200°C (400°F), Gas Mark 6, for 30–40 minutes, or until soft and slightly collapsed. Remove from the oven.

When cool enough to handle, hold each aubergine by the stalk over a bowl and carefully strip off and discard the skin, saving any juice in the bowl. Put the pulp, while still warm, and any juice in a food processor or blender and pulse to mash roughly. Add the garlic, lemon juice and tahini and process to a smooth paste. Season with salt and cayenne and leave to cool, then cover and chill for a few hours before serving.

To serve, put the purée in a shallow dipping bowl and drizzle over some olive oil and cayenne pepper. Serve with the vegetable crudités to dip into it.

Serves 4–6

2 large aubergines
2 garlic cloves, crushed
juice of 2 lemons
1 tablespoon tahini
salt and freshly ground cayenne pepper
olive oil, for drizzling

To serve
red radishes, trimmed
spring onions, trimmed
celery, carrot and cucumber strips

This recipe takes the Egyptian dip baba ghanoush as its inspiration. In Egypt breads and dips are eaten as snacks or as part of the main meal.

Peanut ice cream in filo shells

Put all the ingredients for the ice cream into an ice-cream machine and follow the manufacturer's instructions, then place the ice cream in a shallow, freezer container and freeze until ready to use.

Alternatively, put all the ice-cream ingredients into a large bowl and, using an electric or rotary whisk, beat for 3–4 minutes. Pour this mixture into a shallow freezer container, cover and freeze for 3–4 hours, or until semi-frozen. Remove from the freezer, transfer to a blender and pulse for a few seconds until the mixture is smooth but slushy. Return it to the container and freeze for 2–3 hours, or until almost firm. Repeat the process of blending and freezing twice more, so three times in all.

Meanwhile, make the filo shells (see page 131) and leave to cool completely.

To serve, put the filo shells on a platter. Remove the ice cream from the freezer and leave to soften slightly, then fill each shell. Garnish with chopped peanuts, dust with icing sugar and serve at once.

Makes 20

Ice cream
600 ml (1 pint) ready-made fresh custard
200 g (7 oz) roasted peanuts, finely chopped, plus extra to garnish
few drops of vanilla essence

Filo shells
200 g (7 oz) filo pastry, thawed if frozen
50 g (2 oz) butter, melted
icing sugar, for dusting

Almost half of all the cultivated land in Senegal is devoted to the production of peanuts, which are also known as groundnuts.

66 Sweet potato pone

Boil the sweet potatoes unpeeled for 10–15 minutes until tender, then peel and cut into small cubes.

Line the base and sides of a 23 cm (9 inch) square cake tin with nonstick baking paper. While the potatoes are still warm, stir in the molasses or sugar, butter and cream, then add the ginger, cinnamon, cloves and orange flower water and stir to mix. Beat the egg yolks and stir in. Using an electric or rotary whisk, whisk the egg whites to soft peaks and fold in.

Spoon the mixture into the prepared tin, smooth the top and put in a preheated oven, 200°C (400°F), Gas Mark 6, for 20 minutes. Reduce the heat to 150°C (300°F), Gas Mark 2 and bake for a further 20–25 minutes, or until set and firm to touch. Remove from the oven and leave to cool completely, before turning out of the tin.

To serve, cut the pone into bite-sized diamond shapes or squares and dust with icing sugar, if using.

Serves 4–6

500 g (1 lb) sweet potatoes
75 g (3 oz) molasses or dark brown sugar
25 g (1 oz) butter
3 tablespoons double cream
2 teaspoons ground ginger
1 teaspoon ground cinnamon
pinch of ground cloves
1 tablespoon orange flower water
3 large egg yolks
2 egg whites
icing sugar, for dusting (optional)

Sweet potato and ginger are used extensively in Liberian cuisine. Pone can be served either hot or cold and is eaten as a snack.

Maschi canapés

Cut the cucumbers in half lengthways and, using a small spoon, scoop out and discard the seeds. Cut the cucumber into 20 x 5 cm (2 inch) long pieces or 'boats'. Lightly sprinkle with salt and put them cut-side down on kitchen paper.

Cut the roast beef into small dice and put in a bowl with the rice, dill, tomato and olive oil. Season with salt and pepper and stir to mix well.

To assemble the canapés, put the cucumber 'boats' on a serving platter and stuff each one with a heaped teaspoonful of the beef and rice mixture. Serve at room temperature.

Makes 20

2 large, long cucumbers
50 g (2 oz) sliced roast beef
10 tablespoons cooked white rice
6 tablespoons finely chopped dill
1 tablespoon finely diced tomato
1 tablespoon olive oil
salt and pepper

This recipe is an adaptation of Maschi, which is a traditional Sudanese dish of tomatoes stuffed with beef and flavoured with spices.

ETHIOPIA

70 Lab with toasted flat-bread dippers

Put the curd and feta cheeses into a bowl and mix until fairly smooth.

Heat the butter in a small, nonstick frying pan and when hot and foaming add the onion and garlic. Cook, stirring, for 3–4 minutes over a high heat, then stir in the turmeric, cardamom seeds and cinnamon and cook for 1 minute. Remove from the heat and add the lemon rind. Stir to mix well, then pour this into the cheese mixture and stir to combine. Season well with salt and pepper, garnish with parsley and serve immediately with grilled or toasted flat-bread strips.

Serves 6–8

400 g (13 oz) curd cheese
100 g (3½ oz) feta cheese, crumbled
1 tablespoon butter
2 tablespoons very finely chopped onion
2 garlic cloves, finely chopped
¼ teaspoon ground turmeric
1 teaspoon cardamom seeds
½ teaspoon ground cinnamon
2 teaspoons thinly grated lemon rind
salt and pepper
chopped parsley, to garnish
2–3 flat breads, cut into thin strips and grilled or toasted until crisp, to serve

Lab is an Ethiopian curd cheese, seasoned with a range of herbs and spices. Here we have replicated its particular acid flavour by mixing feta cheese with regular curd cheese.

Oyster Mombasa

Combine all the ingredients for the topping in a small bowl and leave to stand at room temperature for 30 minutes.

Meanwhile, shuck the oysters. Wash the 20 bottom shells and dry with kitchen paper. Line a serving platter with a bed of sea salt, put the oyster shells on it and set aside.

Carefully dip the oysters into the seasoned flour, then into the beaten egg and then into the dried breadcrumbs, to coat evenly.

Heat the oil in a large, deep saucepan to 190°C (375°F) and, working in batches, deep-fry the oysters for 1–2 minutes, or until lightly golden and crisp on the outside (the oysters should remain soft inside). Drain each batch on kitchen paper while you fry the remainder.

To serve, put each fried oyster on each prepared oyster shell and spoon over a little of the garlic and chilli topping. Serve immediately.

Makes 20

20 large fresh oysters
sea salt, for lining platter
6 tablespoons seasoned flour
2 eggs, lightly beaten
200 g (7 oz) natural dried breadcrumbs
sunflower oil, for deep-frying

Topping
2 garlic cloves, very finely diced
2 red chillies, deseeded and very finely
    sliced or diced
3 tablespoons very finely chopped parsley
juice of 3 limes
2 tablespoons light olive oil
salt

Kenya is **renowned** for its **oysters** and this is a **typical** way to **prepare** and **serve** them, either as a **snack** or a **starter**.

74 Cocktail spice island fish cakes

Cook the potatoes in lightly salted, boiling water for about 15 minutes, or until just tender, then drain thoroughly. Put the fish in a food processor or blender and roughly pulse. Add the potatoes to the fish with the spices, lemon rind and juice, season with salt and pepper and process briefly until just combined. Transfer to a bowl and mix to a firm consistency. Divide the mixture into 20 portions and form into balls.

Spread the breadcrumbs on a large plate and roll each ball in them, to cover completely. Put the balls on a nonstick tray and press down lightly on each one to form a cake. Cover and chill overnight.

When ready to cook, lightly grease a baking sheet and line with nonstick baking paper. Transfer the fish cakes to the baking sheet and drizzle over a little oil. Put in a preheated oven, 200°C (400°F), Gas Mark 6, for 10–12 minutes until lightly golden and cooked through, then remove from the oven and leave to cool to room temperature before serving.

Makes 20

200 g (7 oz) potatoes, peeled and roughly chopped
200 g (7 oz) halibut or cod fillet, roughly chopped
1 teaspoon crushed saffron threads
1/4 teaspoon ground cloves
2 teaspoons ground cumin
2 teaspoons ground cayenne pepper
1/2 teaspoon ground coriander
1 teaspoon fennel seeds
thinly grated rind and juice of 1 lemon
natural dried breadcrumbs, for coating
olive oil, for drizzling
salt and pepper

Cloves were the first spice to be introduced to Zanzibar. They thrived and more spices followed, leading to the country's nickname of 'The Spice Island'.

Piri-piri chicken drumettes

To prepare the chicken wings to make the drumettes, cut through the first joint of each wing and discard the wing tips. Holding the small end of the second joint, cut and gently scrape the chicken meat down towards the thick end of the wing. Pull the skin and meat over the end of the bone with your fingers, to resemble a baby chicken drumstick, then, using a sharp knife or kitchen scissors, trim off the knuckle end of the exposed bone. Repeat with the remaining wings. Arrange the wings in a single layer in a shallow, non-reactive dish.

Mix all the ingredients for the marinade and pour over the drumettes. Toss to coat evenly, cover and marinate overnight in the refrigerator.

When ready to cook, line a baking sheet with nonstick baking paper. Put the chicken drumettes on the baking sheet and put in a preheated oven, 180°C (350°F), Gas Mark 4, for 25–30 minutes, or until cooked through. Remove from the oven and serve immediately with wedges of lemon to squeeze over.

Makes 20

20 large chicken wings
lemon wedges, to serve

Piri-piri marinade
4 tablespoons olive oil
2 garlic cloves, crushed
2 teaspoons grated fresh root ginger
4 tablespoons piri-piri sauce or
  hot chilli sauce
1 tablespoon honey
juice of 3 lemons
salt to taste

The **piri-piri** chilli pepper is believed to have been **introduced** to Mozambique by the Portuguese. The word is Swahili and means 'pepper-pepper'.

78 Mini bobotie open pies

Put the pastry on a lightly floured surface and stamp out 24 circles with a 7 cm (3 in) round pastry cutter. Line 24 nonstick mini muffin tin holes with the pastry, pressing it down to fit neatly. Cover and chill in the refrigerator until ready to cook.

Heat the oil in a pan, add the onion, beef and spices and stir-fry over a high heat for 3–4 minutes. Add the tomato purée and beef stock. Bring to the boil, then reduce the heat to low, cover the pan and cook for 10–15 minutes, stirring occasionally, until the meat is just tender and the liquid has evaporated. Season with salt and pepper and set aside to cool.

Spoon teaspoonfuls of the cooled beef mixture into the pastry cases to come halfway up the sides.

Beat the eggs, nutmeg and cream, season with salt and pepper and carefully pour this mixture over the mince to just cover. Place in a preheated oven, 200°C (400°F), Gas Mark 6, for 12–15 minutes, or until the tops are set. Leave the pies to cool for 10 minutes then turn out of the tins and serve.

Makes 24

3 sheets ready-rolled shortcrust pastry, thawed if frozen

flour, for dusting

1 tablespoon olive oil

1 tablespoon finely chopped red onion

200 g (7 oz) minced beef

1/4 teaspoon allspice

1/2 teaspoon ground cinnamon

1/2 teaspoon ground coriander

1 tablespoon tomato purée

50 ml (2 fl oz) beef stock

2 large eggs

pinch of nutmeg

50 ml (2 fl oz) single cream

salt and pepper

South African cuisine has evolved to incorporate elements from the many nationalities who have lived in the country over the years. Bobotie is a popular Cape Malay dish.

ASIA

82 Spicy pea and potato samosas

First make the filling. Heat the ghee or oil in a large, nonstick frying pan. Add the garlic and red chilli and stir-fry for 1 minute, then add the spices and stir-fry for 20–30 seconds. Add the potatoes and peas and stir-fry over a medium heat for 4–5 minutes. Remove from the heat and stir in the fresh coriander. Season with salt and set aside to cool.

Line a baking sheet with nonstick baking paper. Roll out the pastry to a 5 mm (¼ inch) thickness. Using a 12 cm (5 inch) round pastry cutter, stamp out 10 discs. Cut each one in half and form into a semi-circular cone. Overlap and roughen the two edges and wet them to seal. Fill each cone with a little filling, then wet the top and crimp the edges to seal completely. Repeat to make 20 mini samosas.

Place the samosas on the baking sheet, brush lightly with melted ghee or butter and put in a preheated oven, 200°C (400°F), Gas Mark 6, for 20–25 minutes. Remove from the oven and serve warm, with ketchup for dipping, if desired.

Makes 20

350 g (11½ oz) shortcrust pastry, thawed if frozen
a little melted ghee or butter, for brushing

Filling

2 tablespoons ghee or sunflower oil, plus extra for brushing
3 garlic cloves, finely chopped
1 red chilli, deseeded and finely chopped
2 teaspoons cumin seeds
2 teaspoons ground cumin
1 teaspoon ground coriander
¼ teaspoon turmeric
300 g (10 oz) potatoes, boiled until tender and cut into 1 cm (½ inch) dice
200 g (7 oz) fresh or frozen peas
6 tablespoons finely chopped fresh coriander
salt
spicy tomato ketchup, to serve (optional)

Samosas are traditional Indian snacks that combine vegetables and spices in a dough pocket that's fried until crispy.

Onion and gram flour fritters

Place all the ingredients for the dip in a blender and process until fairly smooth. Transfer to a bowl and chill until ready to serve.

Sift both flours into a large bowl and add the spices. Season with salt, then pour in enough cold water – about 200 ml (7 fl oz) – to make a thick, pourable batter. Add the onion slices and mix well until you have a thick mixture.

Pour the oil into a large, deep saucepan to one-third full and heat to 180°C (350°F). Working in batches, carefully lower large teaspoonfuls of the onion mixture into the oil and fry for 3–4 minutes, or until crisp and golden. Remove each batch with a slotted spoon and drain on kitchen paper while you fry the next batch, keeping the fritters warm.

To serve, place the fritters on a platter with the bowl of dip in the centre.

Serves 4–6

225 g (7$\frac{1}{2}$ oz) gram flour or chickpea flour
1 tablespoon rice flour
2 tablespoons crushed coriander seeds
1 teaspoon chilli powder
$\frac{1}{4}$ teaspoon turmeric
2–3 onions, halved and very thinly sliced
sunflower oil, for deep-frying
salt

Coconut and mint chutney dip
100 g (3$\frac{1}{2}$ oz) freshly grated coconut flesh
1 green chilli, deseeded and chopped
small handful of chopped mint
200 ml (7 fl oz) thick natural yogurt
1 teaspoon sugar
1 teaspoon salt

Also known as besan, gram or chickpea flour is used extensively in Indian cooking. It is high in protein, which benefits the largely vegetarian population.

CHINA

86 Steamed Chinese purses

Place all the ingredients for the filling in a food processor or blender and process until well combined. Transfer to a bowl, cover and chill for 4–5 hours or overnight.

Using a 6 cm (2½ inch) round biscuit or pastry cutter, stamp out rounds from each wonton wrapper. Place a heaped teaspoonful of the filling in the centre of a wonton round and press down gently to spread the filling almost to the edges. Place the filled round in the palm of your hand and then cup your hand, pressing the filling down with your thumb to make an open cup or purse. Tap the base gently on a clean surface to make a flat base and neaten the top with your fingers. Repeat to make 20 purses.

Line 3 layers of a bamboo steamer with baking paper and arrange the purses on them. Cover and steam over a wok or saucepan of boiling water for 8–10 minutes, or until cooked through. Serve the purses immediately with soy dipping sauce.

Makes 20

20 fresh wonton wrappers, each 7.5 cm (3 inch) square
soy dipping sauce, to serve

Filling
100 g (3½ oz) minced chicken
100 g (3½ oz) raw prawns, chopped
1 teaspoon crushed Szechuan pepper
1 egg white
1 teaspoon sesame oil
1 teaspoon finely grated garlic
1 teaspoon finely grated fresh root ginger
1 teaspoon dark soy sauce
2 tablespoons finely chopped chives

Steaming is a popular method of cooking in China, and these little 'purses' or buns are well liked.

Salt and chilli squid

Open out the squid tubes and pat dry with kitchen paper. Lay them on a chopping board, shiny-side down, and, using a sharp knife, lightly score a fine diamond pattern on the flesh, being careful not to cut all the way through. Cut the squid into 5 x 2 cm (2 x 1 inch) pieces and place in a non-reactive dish. Pour over the lemon juice, cover and chill for 15 minutes.

Fill a wok one-third full with oil and heat to 180°C (350°F). Combine the cornflour, salt, pepper, chilli powder and sugar in a bowl. Dip the squid pieces into the beaten egg white and then into the cornflour mixture, shaking off any excess.

Deep-fry the squid, in batches, for 1 minute, or until it turns pale golden and curls up. Remove each batch with a slotted spoon and drain on kitchen paper.

Mix all the ingredients for the dipping sauce in a bowl. Serve the squid in small paper cones, if desired, garnished with sliced red chilli and spring onions and accompanied by the dipping sauce.

Serves 6–8

750 g (1½ lb) squid tubes, halved lengthways
200 ml (7 fl oz) lemon juice
100 g (3½ oz) cornflour
1½ tablespoons salt
2 teaspoons white pepper
1 teaspoon chilli powder
2 teaspoons caster sugar
4 egg whites, lightly beaten
sunflower oil, for deep-frying

Garnish
finely sliced red chillies
finely sliced spring onions

Dipping sauce
1 red chilli, deseeded and finely diced
1 tablespoon very finely diced shallot
2 teaspoons very finely chopped fresh coriander
6 tablespoons light soy sauce
1 tablespoon Chinese rice wine

Seafood is eaten with great regularity in China and squid will often be served as a snack or a side dish as part of a meal.

90 Chilli beef and lime lettuce wraps

Heat the oil in a nonstick frying pan or wok and when hot add the beef, garlic, lemon grass, lime leaves, spring onions and chillies. Stir-fry over a high heat for 5–6 minutes, or until the beef is sealed and lightly browned.

Add the soy sauce and stock and bring back to the boil. Cook over a moderate heat for 8–10 minutes, stirring often, until all the liquid has been absorbed. Remove from the heat and leave to cool. When cool, stir in the cucumber.

Mix the lime juice with the fish sauce and sugar and stir until the sugar has dissolved. Spoon this mixture over the beef and toss to mix well.

To serve, arrange the lettuce leaves on a serving platter and spoon 1 tablespoonful of the beef mixture into each of them. Garnish with the chilli and lime leaf slivers and scatter over some chopped peanuts. Serve immediately.

Makes 20

1 tablespoon sunflower oil
250 g (8 oz) minced beef
2 garlic cloves, finely chopped
1 tablespoon finely chopped lemon grass
4 kaffir lime leaves, finely shredded
2 spring onions, finely sliced
2 red chillies, deseeded and finely chopped
1 tablespoon dark soy sauce
100 ml (3½ fl oz) chicken stock
4 tablespoons finely diced cucumber
juice of 2 limes
1 tablespoon Thai fish sauce
1 teaspoon caster sugar
20 small baby gem lettuce leaves

Garnish
slivers of red chilli
kaffir lime leaves, finely shredded
chopped roasted peanuts

Kaffir lime leaves add an intense citrus zing to sweet and savoury dishes.

Fragrant prawn and herb rolls   93

Cut the prawns in half lengthways, devein, clean and set aside. Combine the mint, coriander and spring onion in a small bowl.

Soak the rice paper rounds, one at a time, in a bowl of cold water and leave to soften for 2–3 minutes. Carefully remove, then drain on a clean tea towel and cut each in half.

To assemble the rolls, place a half sheet of rice paper on a clean surface and top with a heaped teaspoonful of the herb mixture and one halved prawn. Fold the rice paper over to enclose the filling, then place another halved prawn, cut-side down, on top and continue to roll into a tight cylinder. Press the ends with a wet finger to seal. Place the roll, seam-side down, on a serving platter and cover with a dampened tea towel to keep moist while you make the rest.

Once prepared, serve immediately with sweet chilli sauce and light soy sauce to dip into.

Makes 20

20 tiger prawns
15 g (½ oz) mint, roughly chopped
15 g (½ oz) fresh coriander, roughly
    chopped
1 spring onion, very finely chopped
10 rounds of rice paper, about 15 cm
    (6 inches) in diameter
sweet chilli sauce and soy sauce,
    for dipping

Rice paper is made not from rice but from the pith of a small Chinese tree. When soaked it becomes strong and pliable.

94 Chilli crab on mini noodle nests

Lightly grease 20 nonstick mini tartlet cases with sunflower oil. Divide the noodles into 20 portions and press each portion into a tartlet case to form a tartlet shape, making sure the base is covered. Lightly brush with more oil and put in a preheated oven, 180°C (350°F), Gas Mark 4, for 8–10 minutes, or until crisp and firm. Remove from the cases and leave to cool on a wire rack.

To make the chilli crab, heat the oil in a large nonstick wok or frying pan and when hot add the spring onions, garlic, ginger and chilli and stir-fry for 2–3 minutes. Add the crab and stir-fry for another 1–2 minutes, then remove from the heat, stir in the chilli sauce and coriander and toss to mix well.

To serve, place a heaped teaspoonful of the chilli crab mixture into each cooled noodle nest and serve immediately.

Makes 20

Noodle nests
100 g (3½ oz) fresh, fine egg noodles
sunflower oil, for greasing

Chilli crab
1 tablespoon sunflower oil
2 spring onions, finely sliced
2 garlic cloves, finely chopped
1 teaspoon finely diced fresh root ginger
1 red chilli, deseeded and finely diced
200 g (7 oz) fresh white crab meat
2 tablespoons sweet chilli sauce
4 tablespoons finely chopped fresh coriander

A **Singaporean favourite** that was **first eaten** in the 1950s when it was **sold** from a small stall. Its **popularity** spread and the dish is **served** in many of the **city's cafés** and restaurants **today**.

Gado gado

Bring a large saucepan of lightly salted water to the boil, add the carrots and long beans and blanch for 2–3 minutes. Drain and refresh in cold water. Cook the potatoes in lightly salted, boiling water for about 15 minutes, or until just tender, then drain and set aside. Arrange all the vegetables on a serving platter with the bean curd.

To make the spicy dipping sauce, combine all the ingredients in a small bowl.

To make the peanut sauce, mix the peanut butter with the chilli and soy sauces and then pour in the boiling water and stir to mix well. Transfer to a dipping bowl.

Serve the vegetables with the two dipping sauces.

Serves 6–8

2 carrots, peeled and cut into thick, 5 cm (2 inch) long fingers
100 g (3½ oz) long beans, cut into 5 cm (2 inch) lengths
2 large potatoes, peeled and cut into thick, 5 cm (2 inch) long fingers
1 cucumber, cut into thick, 5 cm (2 inch) long fingers
200 g (7 oz) ready-prepared fried bean curd, cut into bite-sized cubes

Spicy dipping sauce
2 tablespoons ketjap manis (sweet soy sauce)
4 tablespoons dark soy sauce
1 teaspoon sambal oelek (hot chilli paste)

Peanut dipping sauce
4 tablespoons smooth peanut butter
2 tablespoons sweet chilli sauce
3 tablespoons light soy sauce
50 ml (2 fl oz) boiling water

This typical Indonesian dish is often served garnished with boiled egg and potatoes, making it a more filling main meal.

98 Soba, tobiko and spring onion spoons

Cook the dried soba noodles according to the packet instructions until just tender. Drain and rinse in cold water.

Whisk the soy sauce with the mirin, sesame oil, wasabi and sunflower oil in a bowl until well blended. Add the noodles and toss gently to coat evenly, then stir in the spring onions and toss to mix well.

To serve, divide the noodles into 20 bite-sized portions and twirl each portion with a fork to make a neat nest. Carefully transfer to individual Oriental soup spoons, then, using a teaspoon, garnish each serving with a little tobiko or small salmon roe and serve immediately.

Makes 20

250 g (8 oz) dried soba noodles
4 tablespoons light soy sauce
4 tablespoons mirin (rice wine)
1 teaspoon toasted sesame oil
$\frac{1}{4}$ teaspoon wasabi paste
6 tablespoons sunflower oil
2 spring onions, very finely sliced
25 g (1 oz) tobiko (flying fish roe)
   or small salmon roe

Tobiko is the small, red-orange, crunchy roe of the flying fish, often served with sushi dishes. Here it's a topping for soba noodles, which are made from buckwheat flour.

AUSTRALASIA

102 Damper squares with lemon myrtle

Line a large baking sheet with nonstick baking paper and dust lightly with flour.

Put the flour, lemon myrtle, sugar and salt into a large bowl and pour in the butter. Gradually add the milk and mix to make a medium soft dough.

Pat the dough into a 23 cm (9 inch) square and put it on the baking sheet. Brush with the egg glaze and put in a preheated oven, 200°C (400°F), Gas Mark 6, for 30–35 minutes, or until golden and cooked through. Remove the damper from the oven and leave to cool on a wire rack.

Cut the damper into bite-sized squares and serve accompanied by whipped cream and jam.

Serves 4–6

500 g (1 lb) self-raising flour, sifted

2 teaspoons ground lemon myrtle

2 teaspoons caster sugar

2 teaspoons rock salt

125 g (4 oz) butter, melted

250 ml (8 fl oz) milk

beaten egg mixed with a little milk, for glazing

whipped cream and jam, to serve

Damper is unleavened bread traditionally made by bushmen and baked in hot ashes – this is a modern version. Bush tucker has become a vital part of Australian culture.

Wattleseed and coffee mini ice creams **105**

Put the sugar, coffee and water into a small saucepan and heat slowly until the sugar has dissolved completely, then simmer for 1 minute. Remove from the heat and set aside to cool.

Whisk the crème fraîche, wattleseed and vanilla essence until smooth, then add the cooled sugar syrup and whisk again until well combined.

Freeze in an ice-cream maker, following the manufacturer's instructions, until the mixture is thick and slushy. Alternatively, freeze and beat manually (see page 65). Carefully spoon the slushy mixture into two 10-hole ice cube trays, place in the freezer and freeze until the mixture can support the sticks in the centre, then freeze until firm. (You will have some leftover ice cream, which can be frozen for future use.)

To serve, carefully unmould the mini ice creams and serve immediately.

Makes 20

150 g (5 oz) granulated sugar
1 tablespoon instant coffee dissolved in
   1 tablespoon warm water
300 ml ($\frac{1}{2}$ pint) water
250 g (8 oz) crème fraîche
2 teaspoons ground wattleseed
few drops of vanilla essence

The **wattleseed** is a grain that has been used in cooking by **Aborigines** for over 6,000 years. Native Australian mint or lemon myrtle can be used instead in this recipe.

106 Barbecued crayfish with chilli sauce

First make the chilli sauce. Purée the chillies, garlic, ginger, sultanas, tomatoes and vinegar in a food processor or blender. Tip the purée into a saucepan and add the salt, sugar and water. Bring to the boil, then simmer for 15–20 minutes, until the sauce has thickened slightly. Allow to cool.

Heat a barbecue until the coals are glowing. Arrange the crayfish on a grill rack just above the hot coals and cook for 2–3 minutes on each side. Alternatively, cook the shellfish under a really hot grill for 5–6 minutes, turning once, until done.

Remove the crayfish from the grill and, holding each one between your finger and thumb, twist off the tail. Hold the tail shell between your thumb and index finger, twist and pull off the flat end – the thread-like intestine will come away. Peel the tail. Discard the rest of the body and shells.

To serve, spoon the sauce into a shallow bowl on a platter and arrange the crayfish tails around it.

Makes 24

24 fresh crayfish (yabbies) or tiger prawns
lemon wedges, to serve

Sweet chilli sauce
150 g (5 oz) fresh red chillies, deseeded
6 garlic cloves
1 teaspoon finely grated fresh root ginger
250 g (8 oz) sultanas
200 g (7 oz) canned tomatoes, drained
white wine vinegar
1 teaspoon salt
350 g (11½ oz) caster sugar
150 ml (¼ pint) water

Called **yabbies** in Australia, **crayfish** have a **sweet flavour** and are a **popular addition** to **barbecues**.

Aussie beer-battered fish fingers

Put the flour, salt, pepper, egg, melted butter and beer in a food processor or blender and process until smooth. Transfer to a large bowl and leave to rest for 30 minutes.

Meanwhile, make the tartare sauce. Combine all the ingredients in a bowl and leave to stand at room temperature for 15–20 minutes.

Heat the oil in a large, deep saucepan to 190°C (375°F). Dip the fish fingers into the batter and fry in batches for 3–4 minutes, or until crisp and golden. Drain each batch on kitchen paper.

Serve the fish fingers while they are still warm, with the tartare sauce for dipping.

Serves 4–6

125 g (4 oz) plain flour
1 teaspoon salt
1 teaspoon freshly ground black pepper
1 egg
25 g (1 oz) butter, melted
150 ml (¼ pint) Australian beer
sunflower oil, for deep-frying
500 g (1 lb) thick white fish fillet (cod or
    halibut), cut into thick fingers

Lemon tartare sauce
300 g (10 oz) good-quality mayonnaise
thinly grated rind and juice of 1 lemon
2 tablespoons finely chopped capers
1 tablespoon finely chopped red onion
1 teaspoon lemon myrtle salt (optional)
dash of Tabasco sauce

Beer helps to make a very good batter for deep-frying and this combination of fresh fish and a piquant sauce is simple but delicious. Lemon myrtle salt is available from speciality food stores.

110 Coconut chicken in banana leaves

Put the banana leaf squares into a bowl, pour boiling water over them and leave in the water for 3–4 minutes, then drain and set aside.

Cut the chicken into 20 x 3.5 cm (1½ inch) bite-sized pieces and put in a large, non-reactive bowl. Mix the coconut cream with the garlic, ginger, coriander, lime rind and juice. Season well with salt and pepper and pour over the chicken. Leave to marinate for 2–3 hours.

Line a two-tier bamboo steamer basket with greaseproof paper. Remove the chicken from the marinade and wrap each piece in a banana leaf square to cover completely. Secure with cocktail sticks or skewers. Put the parcels in the steamer baskets and steam over a pan of boiling water for 10–12 minutes, or until just cooked through. Serve warm on the steamer trays, with a bowl for the discarded banana wrappers and cocktail sticks.

Makes 20

20 banana leaf squares, about 6 cm
    (2½ inches) square
2 large, boneless chicken breasts
125 ml (4 fl oz) coconut cream
2 garlic cloves, crushed
1 teaspoon finely grated fresh
    root ginger
1 teaspoon ground coriander
thinly grated rind and juice of 1 lime
salt and pepper

Steaming in a banana leaf keeps the chicken **deliciously tender** and it's a **popular cooking method** throughout the **South Pacific**. The banana leaves are not edible.

Grilled baby rack of lamb cutlets

Trim all the excess fat from the lamb racks and, using a sharp knife, cut each rack into 4 small 'cutlets'. Season well with salt and pepper, put in a shallow bowl and drizzle with the olive oil. Cover and leave at room temperature for 15–20 minutes.

Combine all the ingredients for the butter in a small bowl. Cover and leave in a cool place until needed.

Arrange the lamb cutlets in a single layer on a grill pan and grill under a medium-high heat for 4–5 minutes, turning once, or until cooked to your liking. Transfer from the grill to a warmed serving platter, spoon a little herb butter over each one and serve immediately.

Makes 20

5 baby racks of New Zealand lamb, with
   4 cutlets on each rack
3 tablespoons olive oil
salt and pepper

Rosemary and mint butter
100 g (3½ oz) butter, softened
2 tablespoons very finely chopped
   rosemary
2 tablespoons very finely chopped mint

New Zealand is famous for its top-quality lamb, which is best cooked simply to really enjoy its succulent flavour. Here it is enhanced by rosemary and mint butter.

114 Anzac biscuits

Line 2 large baking sheets with nonstick baking paper. Mix the oatflakes with the coconut, flour and sugar in a bowl. Put the butter and golden syrup or treacle in a small bowl and stir over a low heat until they melt. Mix the baking soda with the boiling water and add to the butter mixture, then stir this into the dry ingredients and mix to combine well.

Drop teaspoonfuls of this mixture on to the baking sheets and press lightly with the tines of a fork. Put in a preheated oven, 160°C (325°F), Gas Mark 3, for 25–30 minutes, or until golden brown, then remove from the oven and put on wire racks to cool. When cool, arrange the biscuits on a platter and serve immediately.

Makes about 48

250 g (8 oz) oatflakes
200 g (7 oz) unsweetened desiccated coconut
250 g (8 oz) plain flour
200 g (7 oz) caster sugar
125 g (4 oz) butter
1 tablespoon golden syrup or treacle
1 teaspoon baking soda
2 tablespoons boiling water

This was **originally** an army issue biscuit that was **essentially** a **substitute for bread**, as it lasted a lot **longer**. Modern varieties are much **more palatable**.

Mini kiwifruit pavlovas

Line a baking sheet with nonstick baking paper. Put the egg whites in a clean bowl and, using an electric or rotary whisk, whisk until softly peaked. Add the sugar 1 tablespoon at a time, whisking well after each addition. Continue to whisk until the mixture is thick and glossy, then fold in the vanilla essence.

Using the tips of 2 teaspoons, put 20 walnut-sized spoonfuls on to the baking sheet, spaced well apart, and, with the back of a teaspoon, make an indent in the centre of each one. Put in a preheated oven, 180°C (350°F), Gas Mark 4, for 5–6 minutes, then reduce the heat to 120°C (250°F), Gas Mark 1/2 and bake for 20 minutes until firm. Allow to cool completely, then lift the meringues from the paper.

Whip the cream and sugar until softly peaked. Put the meringues on a serving platter and place a small teaspoon of cream in the centre of each one, then top with a couple of slices of kiwifruit. To serve, dust the pavlovas lightly with icing sugar.

Makes 20

2 egg whites
125 g (4 oz) caster sugar
drop of vanilla essence
icing sugar, for dusting

Topping
50 g (2 oz) double cream
1 tablespoon caster sugar
1 kiwifruit, peeled and sliced

Kiwi seeds were brought to New Zealand from China in the early 1900s. However, it's the **flightless bird** and not the fruit that's the **national symbol** of the country.

SOUTH AND CENTRAL AMERICA

120 Spinach and pepper quesadilla wedges

Blanch the spinach in a saucepan of boiling water for 1–2 minutes. Drain thoroughly, squeeze out all the excess water and chop finely. Put in a bowl with the peppers, garlic, spring onions and coriander and season well with salt and pepper. In another bowl, mix the mozzarella, Cheddar and soured cream.

Put the tortillas on a clean surface and spread some of the cheese mixture over each one. Carefully spread the spinach mixture over 3 of the prepared tortillas, to come up to the edges of the tortilla. Sandwich this filling with the remaining 3 prepared tortillas, cheese-side down, and press lightly to make 3 stuffed tortilla sandwiches.

Heat a large, nonstick frying pan over a medium-high heat and lightly brush with oil. Put a quesadilla in the pan and, using a spatula, press down lightly while it cooks for 1–2 minutes. Carefully flip it over and cook for 2–3 minutes. Remove and keep warm while you cook the 2 remaining quesadillas. Cut each quesadilla into 8 wedges and serve at once.

Makes 24

200 g (7 oz) baby spinach leaves
200 g (7 oz) bottled roasted red pepper, drained and finely chopped
1 garlic clove, crushed
4 spring onions, very finely chopped
2 tablespoons finely chopped fresh coriander
300 g (10 oz) mozzarella cheese, coarsely grated
150 g (5 oz) Cheddar cheese, coarsely grated
50 ml (2 fl oz) soured cream
6 x 15 cm (6 inch) flour or corn tortillas
olive oil, for brushing
salt and pepper

Quesadillas are just one variation of the tortilla – a flat bread that is used in many typical Mexican dishes.

Chilli and corn muffins with guacamole 123

Lightly grease two 12-cup mini muffin tins with sunflower oil. Put the flour, cornmeal or polenta, baking powder, bicarbonate of soda, cumin seeds, salt, chillies, coriander and sugar in a large bowl. Mix well, then add the egg, buttermilk and butter and fold together to make a slightly wet batter, adding a little more milk if necessary.

Spoon the batter into the prepared muffin tins and put in a preheated oven, 200°C (400°F), Gas Mark 6, for 12–15 minutes, or until risen and golden. Remove from the oven and leave to cool in the tins for 5–10 minutes, before turning out.

Serve the muffins accompanied by bowls of guacamole, soured cream and salsa.

Makes 24

sunflower oil, for greasing

125 g (4 oz) plain flour

65 g (2½ oz) fine cornmeal or polenta

1 teaspoon baking powder

1 teaspoon bicarbonate of soda

2 teaspoons cumin seeds

large pinch of salt

2 red chillies, deseeded and finely chopped

4 tablespoons very finely chopped fresh coriander

1 tablespoon caster sugar

1 large egg, beaten

125 ml (4 fl oz) buttermilk

40 g (1½ oz) butter, melted

To serve
guacamole
soured cream
Mexican salsa

When you eat them, the **heat from chillies** makes your brain **release endorphins**, so the **more chillies** you have, the **happier you'll feel.**

124 Chorizo, tomato and onion empanaditas

First make the filling. Heat the oil in a frying pan and cook the onion gently for 10 minutes, until lightly browned. Crumble the sausage into the pan. Turn the heat to high and stir-fry for 2–3 minutes, then add the tomato, tomato purée and stock. Bring to the boil, then reduce the heat, cover the pan and cook gently for 15 minutes, stirring often, until the mixture is thick. Season with salt and pepper and leave to cool.

Line a baking sheet with nonstick baking paper. Roll out the pastry to a 2.5 mm (⅛ inch) thickness and stamp out 20 circles with a 7 cm (3 inch) round cutter. Put 1 heaped teaspoon of the filling in each circle and fold the pastry into a half-circle. Crimp and seal the edges. Arrange on the baking sheet, brush with egg and put in a preheated oven, 200°C (400°F), Gas Mark 6, for 12–15 minutes, or until golden. Serve at once or at room temperature.

Makes 20

375 g (12 oz) shortcrust pastry
beaten egg, for brushing

Filling
1 tablespoon olive oil
1 large onion, finely chopped
200 g (7 oz) fresh chorizo sausage,
  skinned
1 tomato, finely chopped
1 tablespoon tomato purée
100 ml (3½ fl oz) chicken stock
salt and pepper

These little baked turnovers can contain a variety of ingredients and the exact filling is often the speciality of the stallholder.

Red bean, spring onion and rice cakes **127**

Mix the rice with the beans and spring onions in a bowl, season well with salt and pepper and set aside.

Put the flour, egg and cream in a bowl, season with salt and pepper and stir to make a smooth batter. Stir in the rice mixture and combine thoroughly.

Brush a large, nonstick frying pan with some sunflower oil and place over a medium heat. Working in batches, drop heaped teaspoonfuls of the batter into the hot pan and cook for 2–3 minutes on each side or until golden and cooked through. Remove each batch to a warmed plate while you cook the rest, brushing the pan with more oil if necessary. Serve immediately with tomato sauce or ketchup for dipping.

Makes about 25

10 tablespoons cooked white rice

5 tablespoons canned red kidney beans, drained and roughly chopped

2 spring onions, finely sliced

65 g (2$\frac{1}{2}$ oz) plain flour, sifted

1 large egg, beaten

4 tablespoons single cream

sunflower oil, for brushing

salt and pepper

tomato sauce or ketchup, to serve

A good source of protein and iron, beans are a staple part of the Colombian diet, particularly amongst those communities where meat is scarce.

128 Annatto lamb on red pepper boats

Heat the oil in a saucepan and when hot add the annatto seeds, garlic and lamb. Cook, stirring, over a high heat until the lamb is browned and sealed. Add the oregano, cumin, tomatoes, beer or lager and bay leaf and bring to the boil. Cover the pan, reduce the heat and cook for 20–25 minutes, or until the mixture is thick and the lamb is tender. Season well with salt and pepper and sprinkle in some chopped coriander.

Cut each pepper into 6 wedges, discarding the stalk and the seeds, to form 18 'boats'. To serve, put the red pepper 'boats', cut-side up, on a platter and carefully spoon a heaped teaspoonful of the annatto lamb into each. Garnish with fresh coriander and serve immediately.

Makes 18

1 tablespoon olive oil

1 tablespoon annatto seeds or
   1 teaspoon turmeric

1 garlic clove, crushed

300 g (10 oz) minced lamb

1 teaspoon dried oregano

1 teaspoon cumin seeds

200 g (7 oz) canned chopped tomatoes

50 ml (2 fl oz) beer or lager

1 dried bay leaf, crushed

1 tablespoon chopped fresh coriander,
   plus extra to garnish

3 large red peppers

salt and pepper

Annatto seeds are used extensively in South American cuisine and are often included as much for the orange colour they impart as for their flavour. Turmeric can be used instead.

Tuna ceviche and mango filo tartlets

First make the filo shells. Brush the filo sheets with melted butter and cut them into 60 x 6 cm (2½ inch) squares. Lightly grease 20 mini muffin holes (2 muffin trays) and line each hole with 3 buttered filo squares, placing each one at a slightly different angle, then gently press the filo down into the hole to make a tartlet shell. Put in a preheated oven, 180°C (350°F), Gas Mark 4, for about 8 minutes until golden and crisp, then remove from the oven, gently take the tartlets out of the tins and leave to cool completely.

Meanwhile, combine all the ingredients for the ceviche in a shallow non-reactive dish, cover and leave to marinate for 10–15 minutes.

To serve, put the filo shells on a serving platter and carefully spoon the ceviche into them. Serve the tartlets immediately.

Makes 20

Tartlet shells

200 g (7 oz) filo pastry, thawed if frozen
50 g (2 oz) butter, melted

Ceviche

100 g (3½ oz) very, very fresh tuna
steak, cut into very fine dice
juice of 1 lemon
2 tablespoons very finely chopped
red pepper
4 tablespoons finely diced ripe
mango flesh
2 tablespoons very finely chopped
fresh coriander
salt to taste

The **origin of ceviche** – raw fish marinated in citrus juice – is a hotly disputed topic, with both Peru and Ecuador claiming the dish as their own.

132 Clams with coconut, lime and ginger

Scrub the clams and discard any that are open. Heat the oil in a large, nonstick saucepan and add the onion and ginger and cook, stirring, over a medium heat for 6–8 minutes. Stir in the coconut milk, chilli, lime rind and juice and sugar, season well with salt and pepper and bring to the boil. Stir in the coriander and clams and cook over a medium heat for 5–6 minutes, or until all the clams have opened (discard any that remain closed).

Meanwhile, pour sea salt on to a flat serving platter – this will provide a stable base for the clams.

Remove the clams from the pan with a slotted spoon and discard the top shells. Bring the coconut mixture in the pan to the boil and cook over a high heat until reduced by half. Arrange the clams in their bottom shells on the serving platter and loosen them slightly, to make eating them easier.

Spoon a little coconut sauce over each clam and serve at once. Have finger bowls on hand.

Makes 25

25 fresh, large clams

1 tablespoon sunflower oil

1 onion, very finely chopped

2.5 cm (1 inch) piece of fresh root ginger, finely chopped

200 ml (7 fl oz) coconut milk

1 red chilli, deseeded and finely chopped

juice and thinly grated rind of 2 limes

1 teaspoon caster sugar

5 tablespoons finely chopped fresh coriander

sea salt, for lining platter

salt and pepper

Brazilian cuisine has many specific regional variations and specialities and clams are particularly popular on the coast at Salvador de Bahia.

Pumpkin wedges with pebre sauce

Put all the ingredients for the dipping sauce in a food processor or blender and process until smooth. Transfer to a bowl, cover and leave at room temperature for 2–3 hours to allow the flavours to develop.

Skin and deseed the pumpkin, then cut it into 20 bite-sized wedges. Put the pieces on a nonstick baking sheet and drizzle with olive oil. Season with salt and put in a preheated oven, 220°C (425°F), Gas Mark 7, for 15–20 minutes, or until just tender. Remove the pumpkin from the oven, put it on a platter with the pebre dipping sauce and serve.

Makes 20

½ medium-sized pumpkin
olive oil, for drizzling
salt

Pebre dipping sauce (Chilean hot sauce)
2 tablespoons olive oil
1 tablespoon white wine vinegar
6 tablespoons water
6 tablespoons finely chopped fresh
    coriander
1 small onion, finely chopped
1 red chilli, deseeded and finely chopped
1 garlic clove, crushed
salt to taste

Chile is a land of contrasts, not unlike this dish where sweet roasted pumpkin is served with a spicy dipping sauce.

136 Barbecued beef strips

Place the steak between 2 sheets of clingfilm and, using a wooden mallet, lightly beat to flatten. Remove the clingfilm and cut the beef into 30 strips about 10 cm (4 inches) long and 3.5 cm (1½ inches) wide. Arrange the beef strips in a shallow, non-reactive dish in a single layer.

Mix the bay leaves with the peppercorns, red wine, oil and thyme in a bowl. Pour this over the beef strips and toss to mix well, then cover and marinate in the refrigerator overnight. Soak 30 bamboo skewers in water.

To cook, remove the beef strips from the marinade and thread each one on to a bamboo skewer, then season well with salt and pepper. Position the skewers under a medium-hot grill or on a barbecue and grill for 4–5 minutes, turning once. Serve beef strips immediately.

Makes 30

750 g (1½ lb) beef fillet steaks
2 dried bay leaves, crushed
10 black peppercorns
250 ml (8 fl oz) red wine
6 tablespoons light olive or sunflower oil
3–4 sprigs of thyme
salt and pepper

Beef plays an important role in Argentina, both culturally and economically. The asado, or barbecue, is the cooking method of choice.

CARIBBEAN

140 Piña colada ice cream spoons

Put all the ingredients in a food processor or blender and process until thick and smooth. Transfer to an ice-cream machine and freeze according to the manufacturers' instructions. Turn into a shallow freezer container and freeze until ready to serve.

Alternatively, put the ice cream mixture into a shallow freezer container and place it in the freezer for 2–3 hours, or until the sides of the mixture start to set. Remove the ice cream and whisk with a fork to break up any ice crystals then return it to the freezer for 2–3 hours. Repeat this process twice more, or until the mixture is smooth and firm.

To serve, using a small melon baller or ice-cream scoop, put small scoops of ice cream on to teaspoons and serve immediately.

Makes 500 ml (17 fl oz)

100 ml (3½ fl oz) coconut milk
100 ml (3½ fl oz) pineapple juice
200 ml (7 fl oz) double cream
100 g (3½ oz) icing sugar
2 tablespoons white rum

Rum, the main ingredient in a Piña Colada, was first produced in the Caribbean as a way of using up the by-product of the sugar industry.

Creamy Cuban black bean soup shots 143

Soak the beans in a large pan of water overnight. Drain and return to the pan. Cover with cold water and boil, uncovered, for 2 hours, or until tender, topping up with boiling water as needed. Drain the beans and set aside.

Heat the oil in a large saucepan and fry the onion for 5–6 minutes until softened. Add the garlic, cumin, oregano and mustard and stir-fry for 1 minute.

Stir in the stock and the drained beans and bring to a boil. Reduce the heat, cover the pan and simmer gently for 25–30 minutes. Transfer the soup, in batches, to a food processor or blender and blend until smooth.

To serve, pour the soup into small cups or espresso cups and drizzle a little cream over each one. Sprinkle over some finely diced red pepper and serve immediately.

Makes 20 cocktail soup shots

200 g (7 oz) dried black beans (also
　　known as turtle beans)
1 tablespoon sunflower oil
2 tablespoons finely chopped onion
1 garlic clove, chopped
1 teaspoon ground cumin
1 teaspoon dried oregano
$\frac{1}{4}$ teaspoon mustard powder
750 ml ($1\frac{1}{4}$ pints) vegetable stock
single cream, for drizzling
finely diced red pepper, to garnish

Black beans provide a link to Cuba's lengthy history, as they were first eaten by the native Indian occupants of the island.

144 Spiced banana and coconut bread

Grease and line a 20 cm (8 inch) square cake tin. Using an electric or rotary whisk, cream the butter and sugar in a bowl, then stir in the beaten egg.

Sift the flour and baking powder into a separate bowl and add the spices and salt. Stir into the butter mixture alternately with the bananas. Stir in the coconut, then spoon the mixture into the prepared tin.

Put in a preheated oven, 180°C (350°F), Gas Mark 4, for 50–60 minutes, or until the bread is firm to the touch and golden. Remove from the oven and stand the bread in the tin on a wire rack for 10 minutes before turning out of the tin, then leave to cool completely.

To serve, cut into small squares.

Serves 4–6

100 g (3½ oz) butter, softened, plus extra for greasing
125 g (4 oz) caster sugar
1 egg, lightly beaten
250 g (8 oz) plain white flour
2 teaspoons baking powder
1 teaspoon ground cinnamon
pinch of grated nutmeg
½ teaspoon ground ginger
¼ teaspoon salt
2 ripe bananas, mashed
65 g (2½ oz) desiccated coconut

Bananas and sugar are Jamaica's two biggest exports; however, numerous hurricanes have threatened to annihilate banana production over the years.

Chilli, sweet potato and plantain crisps   **147**

Using a vegetable peeler, cut the sweet potato into very thin, long slices.

Using a sharp knife, peel the plantain and slice it into very thin circles.

Pour the oil into a deep saucepan to one-third full and heat to 180–190°C (350–375°F). Deep-fry the sweet potato and green plantain in batches for 1–2 minutes, or until crisp and golden. Remove each batch with a slotted spoon and drain on kitchen paper. Sprinkle over the salt and chilli powder and serve.

Serves 4–6

1 red sweet potato, peeled
1 green plantain
vegetable oil, for deep-frying
coarse salt, for sprinkling
mild chilli powder, for sprinkling

Unlike bananas, plantains must be cooked before being eaten; however, once cooked they can be eaten at every stage of ripeness, from green to dark brown.

148 Fried yam and pineapple sticks

Peel the yam and cut it into 20 bite-sized cubes. Peel and core the pineapple and cut it into 20 bite-sized cubes.

Heat half the oil in a large nonstick frying pan and when hot add the yam cubes, cayenne pepper and salt. Stir well, then cook over a medium heat for about 10 minutes, or until the yam is lightly browned all over and tender. Remove the yam from the pan and drain on kitchen paper.

Wipe the pan and heat the remaining oil over a high heat. Add the pineapple pieces and stir-fry over a high heat for 2–3 minutes. Remove with a slotted spoon, drain on kitchen paper and keep warm.

To assemble the sticks, skewer a piece of the fried yam with one of pineapple on a cocktail stick or small bamboo skewer. Repeat to make 20 sticks and serve immediately.

Makes 20

750 g (1 1/2 lb) yam
1/2 ripe, sweet pineapple
6 tablespoons sunflower oil
1/4 teaspoon cayenne pepper
salt, to taste

Despite appearances, the yam is not related to the sweet potato. It is a tuber that is grown on vines and there are an astonishing 150 varieties.

Cornmeal and okra squares

Lightly grease 24 nonstick mini muffin holes with sunflower oil. Sift the flour, cornflour and baking powder into a bowl and stir in the cornmeal, thyme, garlic salt, cayenne and oregano. Make a well in the centre and pour in the milk and egg. Stir to mix, then pour in the melted butter and fold in gently. Stir in half the sliced okra.

Spoon this batter into the prepared tins and top each one with a couple of slices of the remaining okra. Put in a preheated oven, 180°C (350°F), Gas Mark 4, for 20 minutes, or until risen and golden. Remove from the oven and leave to cool in the tins for 10 minutes before turning out.

Serve warm or at room temperature with a tomato salsa, if desired.

Makes 24

sunflower oil, for greasing
100 g (3½ oz) self-raising flour
2 tablespoons cornflour
½ teaspoon baking powder
75 g (3 oz) fine cornmeal
1 teaspoon dried thyme
2 teaspoons garlic salt
½ teaspoon cayenne pepper
¼ teaspoon dried oregano
175 ml (6 fl oz) milk
1 egg, beaten
25 g (1 oz) butter, melted
2 okra, very thinly sliced
tomato salsa, to serve (optional)

Okra is native to Africa and it originally found its way to Puerto Rico when slaves brought it with them. It is now an important crop in the country.

152 Papaya, lime and mango tartlets

Roll out the pastry on a lightly floured surface to a 2.5 mm (⅛ inch) thickness, then, using a 5 cm (2 inch) round biscuit or pastry cutter, stamp out 20 rounds. Use the pastry rounds to line 20 x 5 cm (2 inch) mini tartlet tins. Prick the pastry bases with a fork and line each tartlet case with baking paper and baking beans. Put in a preheated oven, 200°C (400°F), Gas Mark 6, for 10 minutes, then remove the paper and beans and return the cases to the oven for 8–10 minutes, or until they are crisp and golden. Remove from the oven.

Put the lime rind in a blender with the cream and condensed milk and pulse until well combined. With the motor running, slowly pour in the lime juice and process until blended. Transfer to a bowl, cover and chill in the refrigerator for 3–4 hours, or until firm.

To serve, put the cases on a serving platter and spoon the lime mixture into each case. Mix the mango with the papaya and, using a teaspoon, fill the cases. Decorate with lime rind and serve immediately.

Makes 20

250 g (8 oz) sweet shortcrust pastry, thawed if frozen

thinly grated rind and juice of 2 large, juicy limes

6 tablespoons double cream

150 ml (¼ pint) condensed milk

2 tablespoons finely diced papaya

2 tablespoons finely diced mango

lime rind, to decorate

The **papaya** is quite a **delicate fruit** and is **best stored** in the refrigerator for a **longer life**. Here, the **tangy lime cream** **contrasts well** with the **sweetness** of the fruit.

Callaloo and Scotch bonnet crostini   **155**

Melt the butter in a large frying pan and add the onion and garlic. Cook over a medium heat for 3–4 minutes, then add the thyme and okra and stir-fry over a high heat for 3–4 minutes. Add the spinach and cook for 3–4 minutes until the leaves have wilted.

Stir in the coconut cream and the chilli, if using, season with salt and stir-fry over a high heat for 1–2 minutes. Remove from the heat and stir in the crab meat. Toss to mix well and set aside.

Lightly grill or toast the bread rounds on both sides and arrange on a serving platter. Put heaped teaspoonfuls of the callaloo mixture on to the toasted bread and serve immediately.

Makes 20

1 tablespoon butter
1 tablespoon finely chopped onion
1 garlic clove, crushed
1 teaspoon chopped thyme
2 okra, thinly sliced
100 g (3½ oz) baby spinach leaves
1 tablespoon coconut cream
1 teaspoon finely chopped Scotch bonnet chilli, deseeded (optional)
4 tablespoons fresh white crab meat
20 small rounds of French bread
salt

Callaloo is a traditional soup from the **island of Barbados**. Here, using the **ingredients** that go into the soup, are **cocktail bites** that capture its flavour.

156 Crisp, sweet-spiced twists

Put the flour and salt in a bowl, add the butter and rub in with the fingertips until the mixture resembles breadcrumbs. Stir in the sugar, cinnamon, caraway seeds, allspice and orange rind. Stir the egg into the pastry to mix a firm dough.

Turn the dough out on to a lightly floured surface and knead for 4–5 minutes, then roll out to a 2.5 mm (⅛ inch) thickness and cut into strips 2.5 cm (1 inch) wide and 15 cm (6 inches) long. Cut a slit at one end of each strip and pull the other end through it to form a loose 'twist'. Repeat with the remaining strips to give 20 'twists'.

Fill a deep saucepan one-third full with oil and heat to 180°C (350°F). Fry the twists, in batches, for 1–1½ minutes, or until golden and crisp. Remove with a slotted spoon and drain on kitchen paper.

Serve the twists warm or at room temperature, lightly dusted with icing sugar.

Makes 20

125 g (4 oz) plain flour, sifted
pinch of salt
25 g (1 oz) butter, chilled and diced
2 tablespoons caster sugar
1 teaspoon ground cinnamon
2 teaspoons caraway seeds
¼ teaspoon ground allspice
1 teaspoon thinly grated orange rind
1 egg, beaten
sunflower oil, for deep-frying
icing sugar, for dusting

Exotic spices are found all over the Caribbean, and are used both in sweet and savoury dishes.

NORTH
AMERICA

CANADA

160 Canadian wild rice-stuffed mushrooms

Line a baking sheet with nonstick baking paper.
Discard the stems of the mushrooms and put the
caps on the baking sheet, gill-side up.

Heat the olive oil in a frying pan over a medium heat
and add the garlic, spring onion and red pepper.
Stir-fry for 4–5 minutes, then add the rice. Cook,
stirring, for 1–2 minutes until well combined, then
season with salt and pepper and carefully spoon this
mixture into the prepared mushroom caps. Sprinkle
the cheese over the mushrooms and put in a
preheated oven, 200°C (400°F), Gas Mark 6, for
10–12 minutes, or until the cheese has melted.
Remove the stuffed mushrooms from the oven and
serve immediately.

Makes 20

20 large button or chestnut mushrooms,
    each about 6 cm (2$\frac{1}{2}$ inches) in
    diameter
1 tablespoon olive oil
2 garlic cloves, finely chopped
1 spring onion, finely chopped
1 tablespoon finely diced red pepper
50 g (2 oz) cooked wild rice
100 g (3$\frac{1}{2}$ oz) Monterey Jack or mild
    Cheddar cheese, finely grated
salt and pepper

Although the name suggests otherwise, wild rice is actually a
grain that's native to Canada. Harvesting is strictly controlled
and must still conform to traditional methods.

Maple-roast duck rolls

Mix the maple syrup with the soy sauce in a bowl and brush on to the duck breast. Put the duck on a baking sheet and roast in a preheated oven, 200°C (400°F), Gas Mark 6, for 15–20 minutes, or until cooked through. Remove from the oven and leave to cool slightly, then, using your fingers, shred the meat into long, thin pieces.

Cut the crêpes or pancakes in half and trim a 5 mm (¼ inch) strip from the rounded edge of each to make 20 straight-sided pieces. Spread some cranberry sauce in the centre of each piece, then top with some of the shredded duck and cucumber and spring onion strips. Roll the crêpes up tightly and secure each one with a chive tie. Put the rolls on a platter and serve immediately.

Makes 20 rolls

- 2 teaspoons maple syrup
- 1 teaspoon soy sauce
- 1 small duck breast, skinned
- 10 ready-made thin savoury crêpes or pancakes, each about 15 cm (6 inches) in diameter
- 3 tablespoons cranberry sauce
- 1 small cucumber, cut into 3.5 cm (1½ inch) long thin julienne strips
- 2 spring onions, cut into 3.5 cm (1½ inch) long thin julienne strips
- 20 long chives, for tying

It was the **Native Americans** who first discovered that the **sap** of the maple tree could be **evaporated**, resulting in a sweet, sticky syrup.

164 Quebec apple dumplings

Melt the butter in a nonstick frying pan and when it is hot and bubbling, add the apple and sugar. Stir-fry for 2–3 minutes, then add the apple juice, raisins, cinnamon and allspice. Cook for 1–2 minutes, or until the apple is just tender, then remove from the heat and leave to cool.

Roll out the pastry on a lightly floured surface to a 2.5 mm (1/8 inch) thickness. Using a 6–7 cm (2½–3 inch) round biscuit or pastry cutter, stamp out 24 rounds. Brush the edges of the pastry rounds with beaten egg and put a teaspoonful of the apple mixture in the centre of each. Fold the rounds in half and, using a fork, press the edges to seal.

Pour the oil into a deep frying pan or deep-fat fryer to a depth of at least 7 cm (3 inches) and heat to 190°C (375°F). Deep-fry the apple dumplings in batches for 3–4 minutes until well browned and crisp. Drain on kitchen paper and dust liberally with icing sugar before serving.

Makes 24

15 g (½ oz) butter

1 large apple, peeled, cored and cut into 1 cm (½ inch) dice

2 teaspoons soft brown sugar

1 tablespoon apple juice

50 g (2 oz) raisins

1 teaspoon ground cinnamon

¼ teaspoon allspice

500 g (1 lb) sweet shortcrust pastry, thawed if frozen

beaten egg, for brushing

sunflower oil, for deep-frying

icing sugar, for dusting

Apples are the most important fruit crop in Canada and Quebec is one of the main apple-growing areas.

Buttermilk-fried onion rings

Put the egg yolks, flour, bicarbonate of soda and pinch of salt in a bowl and beat with a large spoon. Gradually pour in the buttermilk, beating until the mixture forms a fairly smooth batter.

Pour the oil into a deep frying pan or deep-fat fryer to a depth of at least 7 cm (3 inches) and heat to 190°C (375°F).

Separate the onion slices into rings and drop them into the batter. Fry the rings in the hot oil in batches of 7–8, for 4–5 minutes, or until crisp and golden. Drain each batch on kitchen paper. When all the onion rings are cooked, fry them again in batches in the hot oil for a minute or two to heat them through and crisp them. Drain on kitchen paper and serve immediately, sprinkled with salt.

Serves 4–6

3 egg yolks
175 g (6 oz) plain flour
$\frac{1}{2}$ teaspoon bicarbonate of soda
large pinch of salt, plus salt to sprinkle
425 ml (14$\frac{1}{2}$ fl oz) buttermilk
sunflower oil, for deep-frying
4 large onions, about 10 cm (4 inches) in diameter, cut into 1 cm ($\frac{1}{2}$ inch) slices

Buttermilk was traditionally used so as **not to waste** the thick liquid that was left after **churning the butter**.

168 Butterscotch brownies

Base-line a 20 cm (8 inch) square cake tin with nonstick baking paper.

Put the butter and sugar in a saucepan and cook over a low heat, stirring constantly, until the sugar dissolves. Pour this mixture into a bowl and leave to cool until tepid.

Beat the egg and vanilla essence into the butter mixture, then gradually sift in the flour, baking powder and salt. Gently fold in the walnuts and pour the batter into the prepared cake tin.

Put the cake in the centre of a preheated oven, 180°C (350°F), Gas Mark 4, for 25–30 minutes, or until it is firm to the touch. Remove it from the oven and let it cool completely in the tin then turn it out and cut into 16 brownies.

Makes 16

50 g (2 oz) butter
225 g (7½ oz) dark brown sugar
1 large egg
1 teaspoon vanilla essence
50 g (2 oz) plain flour
1 teaspoon baking powder
pinch of salt
100 g (3½ oz) walnuts, roughly chopped

The first published recipe for a brownie appeared in the USA in 1897. It is thought the dense, fudgy squares had been made for some time by women who received the recipe by word of mouth.

Cocktail hamburgers

To prepare the buns, make the dough (see first step on page 172). Lightly flour a baking sheet. Knock back the dough, then divide it into 20 pieces. Shape each one into a round ball, place on the baking sheet and press down to form bun shapes. Cover with a cloth and leave to rise for 20 minutes.

Brush the buns with beaten egg and sprinkle with sesame seeds. Bake in a preheated oven, 200°C (400°F), Gas Mark 6, for 10–12 minutes. Remove from the oven and cool on a wire rack.

Meanwhile, make the burgers. Line a baking sheet with nonstick baking paper. Mix the beef with the apple, onion, Tabasco and salt and pepper until well combined. Divide the mixture into 20 portions. Mould each one into a burger shape and place on the baking sheet. Bake for 10–12 minutes.

To serve, split the buns in half and put the burgers on the bottom halves. Top each burger with ketchup, onion rings and tomatoes. Put the tops on and secure with cocktail sticks.

Makes 20

Burger buns
250 g (8 oz) strong white flour, sifted
pinch of salt
165 ml (5½ fl oz) hand-warm water
2 teaspoons olive oil
1 heaped teaspoon easy-blend dried yeast
beaten egg, for brushing
sesame seeds, for sprinkling
tomato ketchup
small onion rings
sliced cherry tomatoes

Burgers
250 g (8 oz) lean minced beef
1 tablespoon finely chopped apple
1 tablespoon finely chopped onion
dash of Tabasco sauce
salt and pepper

The first **hamburger** chain was started in 1916 in **Kansas**, but it took a **few more years** before the idea really **took hold** in America.

172 New York-style hot dogs

First make the hot dog buns. Put the flour in a bowl with the salt, make a well in the centre and add the water and oil. Sprinkle the dried yeast over the liquid and leave for 2–3 minutes to dissolve. Gently draw in the flour from the sides of the bowl and knead to a sticky dough. Turn the dough out on a floured surface and knead for 10 minutes until elastic and smooth. Place in a bowl, cover with clingfilm and leave to rise in a warm place for 1½ hours.

Lightly flour a baking sheet. Knock back the dough, divide it into 20 portions and shape each one into a cylinder, about 3 cm (1¼ inches) long. Put on the baking sheet, cover and leave to rise for 20 minutes.

Brush each roll with egg and put in a preheated oven, 200°C (400°F), Gas Mark 6, for 10–12 minutes, or until lightly browned and cooked through. Remove from the oven and cool on a wire rack.

To serve, split each roll lengthways along the top. Fill with a cocktail frankfurter or sausage. Pipe over the mustard and ketchup and serve.

Makes 20

20 mini cocktail frankfurters or
   sausages
American-style mustard
tomato ketchup

Hot dog buns
250 g (8 oz) strong white flour, sifted
pinch of salt
165 ml (5½ fl oz) hand-warm water
2 teaspoons olive oil
1 heaped teaspoon easy-blend dried
   yeast
beaten egg, for brushing

The **hot dog** stand is a **quintessential** New York **institution** and one that has been **feeding hungry passers-by** since the late 1800s.

Lobster and tarragon puffs

175

Line a large baking sheet with nonstick baking paper. Roll out the pastry on a lightly floured surface to a 5 mm (¼ inch) thickness. Using a 6 cm (2½ inch) round biscuit or pastry cutter, stamp out 40 rounds. Put 20 of the rounds on the baking sheet, spaced well apart, and brush with beaten egg. Using a 3 cm (1¼ inch) cutter, stamp out circles from the centre of the remaining rounds. Discard the inner pastry circles, leaving you with 20 pastry 'rings'. Put these 'rings' on the brushed pastry rounds and gently press to seal. Brush again with the beaten egg, then put in a preheated oven, 200°C (400°F), Gas Mark 6, for 12–15 minutes, or until risen and golden. Remove from the oven and put on a wire rack to cool completely.

Meanwhile, make the filling. Put the lobster meat in a bowl and mix in the mayonnaise, mustard, red pepper and tarragon. Season well with salt and pepper and, using a teaspoon, carefully spoon into the cold puff shells. Garnish with sprigs of tarragon and serve immediately.

Makes 20

Puff shells
200 g (7 oz) puff pastry, thawed if frozen
beaten egg, for glazing

Filling
150 g (5 oz) lobster tail meat, chopped into 1 cm (½ inch) dice
4 tablespoons mayonnaise
1 teaspoon American-style mustard
1 tablespoon very finely diced red pepper
2 tablespoons very finely chopped tarragon
salt and pepper
tarragon sprigs, to garnish

Lobster wasn't always considered a luxury: when the colonists first settled in New England they thought them a pest and used the meat as fish bait.

176 Blueberry griddle cakes

Sift the flour, baking powder, sugar and salt into a large bowl. Make a well in the centre and pour in the eggs and milk. Using a large spoon, mix just long enough for the mixture to blend, then stir in the butter and blueberries. Don't overmix: the griddle cakes will be lighter if the batter is not too smooth.

Heat a griddle pan or a heavy-based frying pan over a moderate heat until a drop of water flicked on to it evaporates immediately. Lightly grease the pan with a pastry brush dipped in sunflower oil. Using a small ladle, pour in enough batter to form a pancake 5–6 cm (2–2½ inches) in diameter. Cook for 2–3 minutes until small bubbles form, then flip the pancake over and cook for 1 minute on the other side until lightly browned. Repeat, using up the batter and lightly greasing the pan as required.

Serve the griddle cakes on a warmed platter, with drizzled maple syrup and a bowl of whipped cream.

Makes 30–35

225 g (7½ oz) plain flour
2 teaspoons baking powder
2 teaspoons caster sugar
large pinch of salt
3 eggs, lightly beaten
425 ml (14½ fl oz) milk
50 g (2 oz) butter, melted
100 g (3½ oz) fresh blueberries
sunflower oil, for greasing
maple syrup and whipped cream,
  to serve

The **blueberry** is **indigenous** to North America. Before the **Pilgrim Fathers** arrived, **Native Americans** were enjoying these **juicy berries** all year round, thanks to **clever** preservation techniques.

Californian sushi cones

Bring the rice and water to the boil in a pan over a medium heat. Cover tightly, reduce the heat to very low and cook for about 15 minutes, or until the rice is tender. Remove from the heat and leave to stand, covered, for 10–15 minutes.

Put the vinegar and sugar in a small saucepan and cook over a medium heat until the sugar dissolves. Remove from the heat and leave to cool. Spoon the sushi rice on to a platter and drizzle over the vinegar mixture. Scatter with the sesame seeds and toss gently. Cover with a damp cloth. Leave to cool.

Cut the nori sheets into 40 x 6 cm (2½ inch) squares and place shiny side down. Divide the rice mixture into 40 and spread one portion in an even layer over the left half of each nori square. Spread a little wasabi over the rice and top with an avocado slice, a cucumber strip, a mushroom and a kari slice. Roll the nori squares into little cones starting at the left corner. Moisten the edges with a wet finger and extra rice to seal them. Repeat to make 40 cones. Serve immediately with a dipping sauce.

Makes 40

175 g (6 oz) Japanese sushi rice
220 ml (7½ fl oz) water
100 ml (3½ fl oz) rice vinegar
4 tablespoons caster sugar
2 tablespoons roasted sesame seeds
7–8 sheets of nori
2 teaspoons prepared wasabi or hot mustard
2 Haas avocados, peeled, stoned and cut into 40 long slices
1 cucumber, deseeded and cut into 40 x 5 cm (2 inch) julienne strips
40 enoki mushrooms
40 slices kari (pickled ginger)
tamari or soy sauce, to serve

Despite being **sushi**, the **Californian cone** did, in fact, **originate** in California as a **response** to the Western **reticence** towards **eating raw fish**.

180 Chilli-bean burritos

Roughly mash the beans and put in a bowl with the onion, cumin, coriander, chilli and oregano.

Lay the tortillas out on a clean surface and spread 1½ tablespoons of the bean mixture on one half of each tortilla. Roll once to enclose the filling, tuck both ends towards the centre and continue to roll – the burritos should now be 8–10 cm (3½ – 4 inches) long.

Arrange the burritos in a single layer on a nonstick baking sheet, seam-side down, and sprinkle the Cheddar over them. Cover loosely with foil and put in a preheated oven, 180°C (350°F), Gas Mark 4, for 6–8 minutes, then remove the foil and bake for a further 3–4 minutes, or until they are warmed through. Remove the burritos from the oven, cut in half, sprinkle with paprika and serve immediately.

Makes 30

400 g (13 oz) canned red kidney beans, drained
1 red onion, finely chopped
1 teaspoon ground cumin
3 tablespoons finely chopped fresh coriander
1 red chilli, deseeded and finely chopped
1 tablespoon finely chopped oregano
15 small flour tortillas
50 g (2 oz) Cheddar cheese, finely grated
paprika, for dusting

Chillies and corn form the backbone of this fusion cuisine whose popularity has spread around the globe.

Mini Key lime pies

To make the lime filling, pour the lime juice into a bowl and whisk in the rind, egg yolks and sugar. Pour into a saucepan and cook over a low heat for 2 minutes, stirring, or until the sugar has dissolved. Gradually add the butter, stirring, and cook for about 10 minutes until thick and glossy. Remove from the heat, cover the surface with clingfilm to prevent a skin from forming and chill until needed.

Lay the pastry on a lightly floured surface and, using a 6 cm (2½ inch) round biscuit or pastry cutter, cut out 48 rounds and use to line 48 x 3.5 cm (1½ inch) tartlet or mini pie tins. Line each with nonstick baking paper and baking beans. Put in a preheated oven, 180°C (350°F), Gas Mark 4, for 8–10 minutes, then remove the paper and beans and return to the oven for 6–8 minutes, or until crisp and golden. Remove from the oven and leave to cool in the tins.

To serve, spoon a little of the lime filling into each pastry case, dust with icing sugar and decorate with candied lime rind, if using.

Makes 48

150 ml (¼ pint) lime juice

thinly grated rind of 4 limes

6 egg yolks

125 g (4 oz) caster sugar

100 g (3½ oz) chilled butter, diced

4 sheets ready-rolled shortcrust pastry, about 25 cm (10 inches) square, thawed if frozen

icing sugar, for dusting

candied lime rind, to decorate (optional)

Key limes are smaller than **Persian limes** and yellow in colour. Introduced to the **Florida Keys** by early Spanish settlers, the fruit **flourished** and **adopted the name** of its new home.

184 Double chocolate meringue whispers

Line a baking sheet with nonstick baking paper. Put the egg whites in a clean bowl and whisk until softly peaked. Add the sugar 1 tablespoon at a time, whisking well after each addition. Continue to whisk until the mixture is thick and glossy, then fold in the cocoa powder and mint essence until just combined.

Fit a piping bag with a large star nozzle, fill with the meringue mixture and pipe 40 rosettes 3 cm (1¼ inches) apart on the baking sheet. Put in a preheated oven, 120°C (250°F), Gas Mark ½, for about 1 hour, or until crisp and dry. Leave to cool completely before removing from the baking paper.

Put the chocolate in a small bowl and melt over a pan of simmering water, then leave to cool. Whip the cream until softly peaked.

Hold each meringue rosette by its point and dip its base into the melted chocolate. Sandwich 2 of the prepared rosettes with 1 teaspoon of whipped cream and repeat to make 20 'whispers'. Arrange them on a plate and dust lightly with cocoa powder.

Makes 20

2 egg whites
125 g (4 oz) caster sugar
1 teaspoon cocoa powder, sifted
drop of mint essence
100 g (3½ oz) plain chocolate
100 ml (3½ fl oz) whipping cream
cocoa powder, for dusting

Milton Hershey, founder of America's most famous chocolate company, began trading in his home state of Pennsylvania in around 1875.

GLOSSARY

Annatto seed: Small, indented, pyramid-shaped seed of the annatto tree, with a powdery, red-oxide-like covering. The flavour is mild, somewhat peppery and earthy. Annatto seeds are available from Seasoned Pioneers Ltd. (www.seasonedpioneers.co.uk)

Enoki mushroom: A delicate mushroom that grows in clumps of spaghetti-like strands, each with a small, snow-white cap.

Foie gras: Liver, usually from force-fed geese.

Kaffir lime leaf: Glossy, dark green, aromatic leaf, available fresh or dried.

Kirsch: Brandy distilled from cherries.

Lebanese cucumber: Smaller and crunchier than an ordinary cucumber.

Lemon myrtle: Leaves of the lemon tea tree.

Long bean: Also known as yard-long bean, because of its size. Similar to, but more pliable than, a green bean.

Nori: Japanese name for a blade-like red seaweed. Usually sold as a rectangular sheet, it is the most commonly eaten alga in Japan.

Plantain: A tropical fruit similar to a banana, but larger and with green skin.

Scotch bonnet chilli: A small, hot chilli named from its resemblance to a Scottish hat.

Sushi rice: Short-grained rice.

Tahini: A thick paste made from ground sesame seeds.

Tamari: Similar to, but thicker than, soy sauce, tamari is a dark sauce made from soya beans.

Tiger prawn: Distinguished by black-and-white stripes across its belly, which turn dark red when cooked.

Wasabi: Japanese version of horseradish, from the root of an Asian plant. Available as ready-made sauce or in powdered form.

Wattleseed: From the Australian wattle tree, the seeds have a coffee/chocolate/hazelnut flavour and are dark brown.

INDEX

ACKNOWLEDGEMENTS

192

Executive Editor Sarah Ford

Editor Jessica Cowie

Executive Art Editor Geoff Fennell

Designer Janis Utton

Photographer Stephen Conroy

Food Styling Sunil Vijayakar

Styling Liz Hippisley

Picture Research Jennifer Veall

Senior Production Controller Martin Croshaw

Picture Acknowledgements

Special Photography © Octopus Publishing Group Limited /Stephen Conroy

Other Photography:

Alamy/Sue Cunningham Photographic 133; /Robert Harding Picture Library Ltd. 20; /Gavin Hellier 16; /David Norton Photography 92; /RogerPix 44

Corbis UK Ltd/Patrick Bennett 165; /Barnabas Bosshart 68; /Jan Butchofsky-Houser 22; /David Cumming; Eye Ubiquitous 145; /Ric Ergenbright 27; /Owen Franken 48; /Stephen Frink 150; /Paul Hardy 39; /Jon Hicks 11; /Robert van der Hilst 122; /Jeremy Horner 142; /Kit Houghton 137; /Rob Howard 71; /Mark A. Johnson 79; /Wolfgang Kaehler 7; /Bob Krist 170; /David Lees 52; /Jean-Pierre Lescourret 32; /Michael S. Lewis 161; /Ludovic Maisant 149; /Lance Nelson 103; /Charles O'Rear 96; /M L Sinibaldi 54, 178; /Pablo Corral Vega 129, 134; /Patrick Ward 60; /Alison Wright 157

Eye Ubiquitous/Liz Barry 28; /James Davis Travel Photography 82; /Julia Waterlow 63

Getty Images/Jerry Driendl 185

Caroline Jones/108, 115, 166

Panos/Mark Henley 86; /Marc Schlossman 76